Fundamentals of
School Marketing

Fundamentals of School Marketing

Johanna M. Lockhart

ROWMAN & LITTLEFIELD
Lanham • Boulder • New York • London

Published by Rowman & Littlefield
A wholly owned subsidiary of The Rowman & Littlefield Publishing Group, Inc.
4501 Forbes Boulevard, Suite 200, Lanham, Maryland 20706
www.rowman.com

Unit A, Whitacre Mews, 26-34 Stannary Street, London SE11 4AB

British Library Cataloguing in Publication Information Available

Library of Congress Cataloging-in-Publication Data
Names: Lockhart, Johanna M., 1971-
Title: Fundamentals of school marketing/Johanna M. Lockhart.
Description: Lanham, Maryland : Rowman & Littlefield, 2016. | Includes
   bibliographical references.
Identifiers: LCCN 2016028741 (print) | LCCN 2016030912 (ebook) |
   ISBN 9781475829952 (cloth : alk. paper) | ISBN 9781475829969 (pbk. : alk. paper) |
   ISBN 9781475829976 (Electronic)
Subjects: LCSH: Schools—United States—Marketing.
Classification: LCC LB2847 .L638 2016 (print) | LCC LB2847 (ebook) | DDC
   338.4/337—dc23
LC record available at https://lccn.loc.gov/2016028741

∞™ The paper used in this publication meets the minimum requirements of American National Standard for Information Sciences—Permanence of Paper for Printed Library Materials, ANSI/NISO Z39.48-1992.

Printed in the United States of America

Contents

Preface

Several years ago, at the request of school administrators in the Houston Independent School district, I created a workshop, *Marketing Your School*. The administrators who attended were aware that the landscape for public schools was changing, and they wanted practical tools and skills to control the new environment rather than be controlled by it.

The success of the *Marketing Your School* workshops led to a subsequent program, *Building Beneficial Partnerships*. As I conducted these workshops over several years, participants repeatedly expressed a desire for a user-friendly guidebook to help them as they implemented their marketing and public relations initiatives.

Four years ago I wrote *How to Market Your School* to meet that need. Subsequent phone calls and e-mails from individuals who had purchased my book made it clear to me that, in addition to public schools, private, charter, faith-based, and international schools also found the book useful for developing and improving their marketing skills. I also realized that my book was now more than four years old and in need of updating, especially in the area of utilizing technology and social media to market more effectively.

A final consideration was to make the book more affordable to schools by creating two books: one for schools wishing to create and maintain a marketing program and one for schools wanting to enhance the effectiveness of an existing one.

Fundamentals of School Marketing covers marketing fundamentals and marketing communication. This book is designed to help schools establish and maintain a marketing program. The marketing communication chapter covers the essential elements of effective communication, a component essential to successful marketing. *Maximize Your School Marketing* covers the fundamentals of media, community, and public relations, fund raising, and social media. This book is designed to enhance an existing marketing program through greater internal and external outreach efforts.

With these two books, I hope to address the needs of all types of schools. If it sometimes seems that I have given public schools more attention, it is simply because they vastly outnumber other types of schools and, more importantly, they are not as practiced in the art of school marketing as private, charter, or faith-based schools.

The present environment for all types of schools is more competitive than in the past. Schools are competing not only for students but also for teachers, administrators, and community support. Students, parents, employees, and members of the community are now "customers" who can choose whether or not to attend, work in, and support a school. Their choices are determined by how they view education in general and their local schools in particular. Marketing, communication, and public relations help shape those views.

Successfully marketing a school involves a concerted effort that includes public relations, media relations, relationship management, and communication. However, often school administrators are not familiar with these fields. Do not despair. The information in *Fundamentals of School Marketing* can help you get started. If you already have a marketing effort, *Maximize Your School Marketing* will facilitate improvement of what you are already doing. Whatever your goals are, I hope one or both these books will become worn from use.

Acknowledgments

I extend my sincere gratitude to those who shared their time, talents, knowledge, and experiences with me.

Hector Rodríguez, Principal, John Herrera Elementary School, Houston, Texas

R. Neal Wiley, Fine Arts Director, Houston Independent School District

Joanie Haley, Executive Director, The McNair Foundation

Elaine Naleski, Director of Community Relations, Colorado Springs School District 11

Special appreciation and thanks to Carol Marcott, a treasured friend, a supportive mentor, a wise advisor, and a motivating cheerleader, and to my son, John Lockhart, who has assisted me in immeasurable ways to make this second edition and my website possible.

Introduction

When I conduct workshops or consult with school administrators and their staff members, most of the participants embrace the marketing concept with enthusiasm, but others struggle against it. Marketing was not part of the job description when they chose to enter education. However, whether those in schools view the idea of marketing as exciting or bothersome, the need to market is not going away. If anything, the need will grow.

Actually, most schools already are marketing to some degree whether they call it that or not. Anytime a school seeks to improve its products and services, reach out to the community in positive ways, or communicate more effectively with its internal and external audiences, it is marketing. What many schools lack is the ability to maximize their efforts through an organized, strategic process.

When looking for guidance, school administrators often hear advice such as, "You need to have an effective brochure," or "The first thing to do is develop a good marketing plan." Other marketing advice stresses that utilizing public relations, developing media relations, conducting research, strengthening community partnerships, and implementing effective communication strategies are equally essential to any marketing effort. However, information to help school administrators know exactly how to do these things is somewhat limited.

Of the numerous marketing books, presentations, and seminars available, few address marketing for educational institutions, especially schools. Most educators have neither the time nor the desire to decipher how to apply private sector marketing information to their particular school situations.

Fundamentals of School Marketing is designed to help school administrators apply the knowledge and tools used successfully in the private sector to organize, implement, and maintain an integrated marketing program that achieves their particular goals. Success in any complex endeavor requires an understanding of the fundamentals. Likewise, successful school marketing requires an understanding of the basic principles of integrated marketing.

Integrated marketing is an approach that recognizes activities such as public relations, media relations, communication, advertising, and relationship management as integral parts of the marketing effort. Benefits include a more efficient use of resources, improved communication, and better coordination of activities.

Fundamentals of School Marketing presents the basics of integrated marketing without jargon, theory, or debate over the merits of the latest marketing trend (although they may be mentioned). However, to implement a marketing strategy, school administrators need to know how to apply those fundamentals effectively to the specific environment of their schools. Most of the content is presented through succinct explanations of the many ways that administrators can develop, implement, and maintain an ongoing marketing program to promote their schools internally and externally. I chose this format because administrators in my workshops indicated that they do not have time to read the traditional text format to extract ideas and activities they can use. Having the information in manageable "chunks" they could read quickly was appealing.

Fundamentals of School Marketing organizes the content into four chapters. Chapter 1, "School Marketing: What It Is and Why It Matters," provides a definition of marketing as it applies to schools, speaks to the influences that make school marketing essential, and describes the benefits of an effective marketing program. Even administrators who are convinced of the importance of marketing should find this chapter helpful if they must persuade less enthusiastic internal staff members, board members, and community partners of the importance of making a commitment to the school's marketing efforts.

Building the foundation of a marketing program is described in chapter 2, "Getting Started." A systematic, well-informed start is the most critical step in any marketing strategy. Marketing efforts will be disorganized and unproductive without a sound beginning. A sound beginning requires knowing exactly where you are and where you want to go and having a strategy and the resources to make the transition. Chapter 2 provides a systematic model to help administrators avoid some of the most common marketing mistakes that result from inadequate planning and lack of focus. Conducting market research and maintaining a database are activities that can enhance marketing efforts. Without proper research, your marketing strategy may be based on faulty perceptions. Chapter 3, "Marketing Research and Database Marketing," provides guidelines for determining when research is warranted and how to conduct various research activities such as surveys, interviews, and focus groups. This chapter also shows the advantages of using a database to target specific audiences, personalize messages, and promote proactive communication.

Communication is the lifeblood of any marketing effort. Whether written or spoken, verbal or nonverbal, channels of communication strongly influence the impression people have of your school. Effective communication must be receiver-sensitive and reciprocal. Too often, the sender bases his communication on what he wants to say rather than what the receiver wants to know. In addition, a successful marketing strategy must create avenues for reciprocal communication with various audiences. Chapter 4, "Marketing Communication," looks at the essentials of receiver-based communication, offers ways to improve two-way interaction, and provides guidelines for creating effective communication materials.

The final portion offers three Success Stories to provide valuable insight from education administrators who have been successful in marketing-related initiatives and were willing to share their experiences and expertise. I have included their stories not only to serve as real-life examples, but also to inspire and motivate.

Once you launched your marketing initiative, you may wish to maximize your efforts with the companion book, *Maximize Your School Marketing*, which covers the subjects (1) Technology and Social Media, (2) Dealing with the Media, (3) Building Better Partnerships, (4) Public Relations, Inside and Out, and (5) Fundraising.

ABOUT THE AUTHOR

Since I will be guiding you through the marketing process, you may want to know something about me. I have over 15 years of experience in marketing and public relations in the private sector that run the gamut from regional director for a public relations firm that represented resort conference centers to director of marketing for an investment firm that specialized in oil and gas securities. What I came to realize is that no matter what the industry, the underlying marketing principles are the same.

For more than 10 years, as Manager of Marketing and Client Relations in the Office of Marketing and Business Development at the Houston Independent School District, I had the opportunity to apply those principles to the department's marketing efforts and to develop marketing workshops for schools. To date I have presented the *Marketing Your School* and the *Building Beneficial Partnerships* workshops to more than a thousand school administrators. In addition, I have spoken on school marketing at state and national levels.

In 2014, I retired from the school district and have launched a new endeavor. My website, *marketyourschool.net*, is a result of feedback from readers of the first edition of my book. It will allow me to provide the assistance to schools, public, private, charter, or parochial anywhere in the country or abroad. The goal is to provide more assistance in different mediums and be more interactive with schools that realize the benefits of marketing.

My academic career includes a Bachelor of Arts in languages and a Master of Arts in communication. As an undergraduate student, I had the opportunity to study in Mexico, Spain, Germany, and England. My experiences in other countries made me acutely aware of the importance of recognizing, understanding, and respecting the differences that exist between groups while utilizing the commonalities to mutual advantage. Through my professional and academic experiences, I have become convinced that knowing your various audiences and being able to communicate with a valid knowledge of *their* expectations is key to successful marketing.

Chapter 1

School Marketing

What It Is and Why It Matters

School marketing is applying the principles of integrated marketing used successfully in the private sector to the increasingly competitive environment of primary and secondary education. As discussed in the Introduction, integrated marketing includes activities such as public relations, communication, advertising, media relations, and any other activity that can help school administrators successfully promote their schools internally and externally.

WHAT SCHOOL MARKETING IS AND WHAT IT IS NOT

School marketing is a way of doing things that expresses to students, parents, school staff, and the community that the school is dedicated to serving the educational needs of the community to the highest degree possible. This includes activities and materials that consistently and effectively promote the school as the best education choice for students and parents, an asset within the community, and a responsible administrator of taxpayers' or supporters' money.

Activities include all the things the school does to develop, implement, and maintain effective marketing, public relations, and communication strategies. Materials include the brochures, videos, newsletters, prospectuses, school website, and social media applications that support marketing activities.

However, marketing is more than activities and materials; it is a way of thinking, a state of mind, an attitude. Believing in the value of marketing, especially in the early stages of the marketing effort, is a critical element for success. Some views about marketing often found among school administrators and staff can sabotage a marketing effort.

One detrimental view is that marketing is just one more onerous task imposed upon school administrators and employees. "In addition to all the other things we are expected to do, now people are telling us we have to spend time marketing ourselves," administrators often complain. Yes, marketing does require time and effort, but the rewards of a successful marketing effort are well worth the investment. An effective marketing program can significantly decrease the time school administrators spend on dealing with disgruntled parents; recruiting volunteers, teachers, and staff; finding additional resources; and building community support.

A second detrimental view is that marketing education is a distasteful activity that is not relevant to educating children. If you feel this way, consider that universities and colleges, institutes and trade schools, and private, faith-based, charter, and for-profit schools have been marketing themselves successfully for some time. Public and private schools in Great Britain, New Zealand, and Australia consider marketing programs essential to creating viable institutions. The truth is, every time you make improvements that enhance the learning environment, increase the attractiveness of the physical surroundings, or seek to improve community relations, you are thinking in the same way marketing professionals do when they develop marketing activities. You are making your school more attractive to your students, parents, employees, and supporters, who are your current and potential "customers."

Successful school marketing is about meeting the needs and desires of internal and external audiences and receiving value in return—an exchange that benefits both sides in increasing proportion. Determining the *needs* and *desires* of an organization's various customers or stakeholders is an essential part of any marketing strategy. For schools, the need already exists. We need to provide our children with the means to receive an education. The law requires it. A school's marketing strategy will focus on the public's desires and expectations. The goal of the marketing effort is to create an educational organization to which parents want to send their children, in which qualified staff want to work, and for which there is community support. The value that the school receives in return for meeting the needs and desires of internal and external audiences may be increased enrollment, quality teachers, contented employees, greater parent participation, more volunteers, improved community support, and beneficial relationships with external organizations. The equation is mutually beneficial and sustaining.

Equally important to understanding what marketing is, is understanding what it is not. These common misconceptions can undermine a marketing effort, waste resources, and create ill will. Before beginning the marketing effort, it is important to ensure that everyone has an awareness of what marketing is not.

School marketing is not an *ad hoc* activity. Have you ever had an acquaintance or relative who called you only when he needed help? After a while you probably avoided him. If a school continuously ignores its stakeholders until a need or crisis arises, the response is likely to be negative. Marketing is not an effort initiated in response to a crisis, concern, or need, then abandoned once the issue is resolved. Marketing should be an ongoing undertaking that is incorporated into the daily actions and thinking of all school personnel. To do otherwise, wastes resources, weakens future marketing efforts, and conveys the idea that the school responds to its stakeholders only when compelled to do so.

School marketing is not hype or spin. When marketing is used as an attempt to obscure the school's inability or lack of willingness to meet the needs and wishes of its stakeholders (students, parents, employees, community), the result is the loss of credibility not only for the school's marketing efforts, but also for any subsequent efforts to meet stakeholder needs. Credibility is essential to every aspect of a marketing initiative. Once creditability is lost, it is difficult to regain.

School marketing is not sales. To many people, marketing and selling are the same. They are, however, significantly different.

Marketing activities are strategic, comprehensive, and indirect. In the private sector, marketing includes multiple phases of activities such as forecasting, product development, position assessment, market research, branding, creation of communication materials, and public relations that enhance the company's long-term relationship with its customers or stakeholders.

Sales is a short-term, direct, operational activity that is a part of the marketing process. In school marketing, sales-oriented activities generally include one-on-one interaction with prospective students or their parents, presentations to community groups, requests to external groups for support, and promotion of special programs or initiatives. Sales efforts are much easier when the marketing initiative is based on a thorough understanding of and a desire to meet your audience's expectations.

Peter Drucker, a recognized management expert, wrote that the aim of marketing is to make sales superfluous.[1] The goal is to know and understand your customers so completely that the product or service fits their needs and desires perfectly. Then, one needs only to let them know that the product or service exists and how to get it.

An often cited example of the accuracy of this viewpoint is the marketing of Cabbage Patch dolls in the 1980s. The marketing strategy for these dolls was so effective that "selling" became a matter of letting customers know when and where they were available. People waited in line for hours to get one. In some instances, police had to control the crowds.

Created by Xavier Roberts, each doll looked a little different from any other and had its own name, birthday, and birth certificate. The dolls were "adopted" from the maternity ward at Babyland General Hospital in

Cleveland, Georgia. The idea and the resulting product and promotion were perfectly attuned to the consumer, children. Children loved the idea of adopting their own, one of a kind, doll.[2]

Consider how in tune technology companies are with their consumers. They ask, they listen, and they create products based on understanding their audiences.

When a school makes an effort to understand its audiences and fulfill their desires to the best of its ability, having to "sell" the school becomes less important than creating an awareness of what the school has to offer.

School marketing is not a department. In his excellent book, *Selling the Invisible*, Harry Beckwith emphasizes that marketing is not a department.[3] The idea is that everyone in an organization is part of the marketing effort. Marketing is about perception, and everyone in an organization is responsible for how the organization is perceived.

When I was an undergraduate student, I worked my way through school as the evening manager at a luxury hotel. The hotel had a well-trained and motivated marketing staff that spent significant time and money promoting the hotel to companies nationwide. However, the hotel reception staff, who interacted with the guests on a daily basis, ultimately determined how the hotel was judged. If the service had been poor, even the best marketing efforts would not have produced repeat business. The loyalty of our guests was maintained in large part by the excellent customer service provided by frontline employees.

Likewise, school marketing efforts can be undermined by unhappy employees, apathetic students, and indifferent parents. However, when properly motivated, these groups can bring tremendous energy, expertise, and support to activities that promote a positive image of the school.

Bus drivers, office staff, crossing guards, custodians, and cafeteria workers should be aware that they are representatives for the school as much as administrators and teachers. This is a very important concept: so important that the phrase *"Everyone is in Marketing"* should be the mantra of a school's marketing effort.

As your marketing efforts succeed, there is an increased sense of pride and accomplishment within the school that is concomitant with success. This pride should be felt by everyone, because each has contributed to that success and each is affected by it.

WHY IS MARKETING YOUR SCHOOL IMPORTANT?

The fact that you are reading this book indicates that you are open to the idea that marketing can provide benefits to your school. Colleges, universities, and vocational and private schools have been marketing to varying degrees for decades. Public schools may not yet need the kind of heavy advertising and promotion activities that these learning institutions do, but the changing environment of public education warrants a proactive approach.

Below are some important changes in the last several decades that affect the climate in which schools must survive. They provide a good argument for serious consideration of a school marketing program. If you are already convinced that marketing is important, use the information presented here to bolster your arguments to unconvinced administrators, motivate school staff, or recruit volunteers to assist you.

- Increased Competition. The number and kinds of schools competing for students have increased dramatically. In the past, private schools and faith-based schools were the only competition for public schools. Decisions for sending children to such schools were generally based on tradition, desire for a particular curriculum or teaching methodology, or a preference for a specific religious environment.

  Today, charter schools, home schooling, for-profit schools, voucher programs, and, in some cases, even schools within the same district may compete for students. With so many choices available, becoming the school of choice is a matter of survival for many schools. Chances are your competition already is marketing to your present and potential students. Marketing is essential to managing the competition by positioning your school as the preferable choice.

  In public schools, loss of students can significantly decrease a school's funding. According to the National Center for Education Statistics, in the school year 2010–2011, average expenditure per pupil was $11,184.[4] Consequently, for a public school, losing fewer than a dozen students can mean a loss of revenue, which is roughly equivalent to salaries for two teachers.

  When other schools take your students, they take not only the funds attached to those students, but also the parental, voter, and community support that is needed in advancing school initiatives. Loss of one student loses the support not only of parents, but possibly grandparents and other relatives who live, vote, and pay taxes in the community.

  However, competition need not be anathema to a school's survival. The key is to look at competition as a catalyst that creates new vigor, innovation, and higher expectations within your school.
- Changing Demographics. Over the past few decades, the demographic landscape has changed significantly and the changes are having an impact on schools. Of major influence are changes in the family structure, increased diversity, and a shift in the adult/child ratio.

One-parent families and those with both parents working are the norm in public school districts. Parents may have less time and inclination to become involved in the education process and even in their own children's activities.

Handling new noninstructional responsibilities, getting working parents involved, and replacing the volunteer services stay-at-home mothers previously provided often tax the resources of schools and the dedication of school staff. Marketing can help you assess the needs of your particular community, find additional resources, and create programs that adjust to societal changes without diminishing the educational experience of the children.

Racial and ethnic diversity among the student population is significantly greater than in the 1950s and 1960s. According to childstats.gov, the percentage of all children living in the United States with at least one foreign-born parent rose from 15 percent in 1994 to 24 percent in 2012. This creates special challenges within both the school and the community.

Diverse customs and languages can present obstacles to student assimilation, parent participation, and two-way communication. A sense of alienation or exclusion may cause parents to avoid contact with the school or to seek other educational opportunities for their children. Both the children and the valuable contribution of cultural diversity are lost to your school.

An important element of an effective marketing effort is a culturally sensitive and inclusive environment for students and parents that avoids alienation and fosters a sense of belonging and school loyalty. Any marketing strategy in a culturally diverse school should include outreach programs that encourage and facilitate not only parent but also community participation.

Another significant change is the shift in the child-adult ratio. Unlike the 1950s and 1960s when children outnumbered adults, today, there are considerably more adults than children in the United States. Many of these adults do not have children in elementary and secondary schools. A school district near where I live reports that 80 percent of the residents in the district do not have children in school.

The influence of these groups is so significant that marketing and advertising groups have created acronyms for them: OINKs (one income, no kids), DINKs (double income, no kids), LINKs (low income, no kids), POOKs (parents of older kids), WOOFs (well-off older folks), and FISTs (fixed income senior taxpayers). For young adults, who plan to have children, the quality of schools is an issue. Older adults and those who do not plan to have children want to feel that their tax dollars are being spent responsibly.

Because they vote, pay taxes, and participate in civic associations, building support among these groups is important. An effective marketing plan can build and maintain positive lines of communication with these groups and create a perception that the school is a positive contributor to the community that is worthy of their tax dollars.

In addition, retired residents are often some of a school's best and most dedicated volunteers. They may serve as mentors, advisors, and goodwill ambassadors for the school. Retired business people may have valuable knowledge or services to share related to your marketing program.

- Public Skepticism. Nearly twenty years ago, the National Commission on Excellence in Education published its now famous—some would say infamous—report on the condition of public education, entitled "A Nation at Risk."[5] The criteria and degree of objectivity the commission used to examine and assess the public education system are still a matter of debate. Whether justified or not, the findings and recommendations of the commission generated a high level of scrutiny and criticism of public schools, which ultimately fostered more scrutiny of U.S. education in general. Much of that criticism lingers today.

  Higher standards, greater accountability, teacher salaries tied to performance, and more stringent graduation requirements for students were some of the commission's recommendations. A significant portion of school administrators and the public supported these requirements. Unfortunately, schools became the scapegoat for many of society's ills. Some groups used the assault on public education to foster their own interests such as charter schools, for-profit schools, home schooling, and voucher programs. Schools, both public and private, now face the task of maintaining and, in some cases, rebuilding public confidence while dealing with a changing society.

  However, increased examination of school performance has had a positive side. Greater public demands have caused schools to be more aware of how the public perceives them. Marketing provides the opportunity to dispel "myths" that have developed about the education system in the United States and inform the community of schools' accomplishments and contributions.

- Media Scrutiny. No news is good news to many school administrators. Many educators feel that negative media coverage contributes to the decline in public confidence in schools and that the media is more likely to cover the negative rather than the positive items.

  School administrators complain that local news reporters often use exposure of inefficiencies within their school districts as major items on the evening news, but do not give the same prominence to school achievements.

The negative implication of national news items such as isolated incidents of school violence spills over to the entire education system.

It should be recognized, however, that school administrators have played a part in the adversarial relationship with the news media. Administrators often are perceived by the news media as uncooperative and obstructive. Stonewalling the media has become the *modus operandi* of many school communication offices. The result is a downward spiraling of effective communication and relations on both sides.

Without proactive measures to build positive relations, interactions with the media can become negative and reinforce unfavorable opinions on both sides. Therefore, an important part of any marketing program is media relations. An effort to build and maintain constructive relations with the news media will pay off when there are both positive and negative events at your school.

- Scarce Resources. There are never enough resources to do all that schools would like to do. At the same time that government mandates and public pressure are placing greater demands on schools, the resources to meet those demands are becoming increasingly difficult to find. Having stretched their budgets to the limit, school administrators spend much of their time determining how to provide more services with fewer resources. Additional resources exist in every community. Accessing them should be a part of the school's marketing plan. Businesses and local organizations benefit when the schools in their area are good; therefore, local businesses are more willing to support schools when they see them as assets within the community. By designing marketing programs that build and maintain supportive relationships in the community, your school can receive extra funds, services, and assistance.

People are attracted to success. That is why attendance increases at sporting events when the home team is winning. As the achievements of your school are recognized through marketing activities, high-quality teachers, reliable staff, and motivated students are more easily attracted and retained. As these groups are attracted to the school, they raise the level of achievement and success.

The benefits of successful school marketing are many. Effective marketing can positively affect virtually every aspect of a school. The most important result, however, of effective school marketing is that it creates an enriched learning environment for all students.

NOTES

1. Drucker, Peter F. *The Essential Drucker: The Best of Sixty Years of Peter Drucker's Essential Writings on Management* (New York: Collins Business Essentials, 2008).

2. "Whatever Happened to Cabbage Patch Dolls?" collectdolls.about.com/library/weekly/aa090101a.htm.

3. Beckwith, Harry. *Selling the Invisible: A Field Guide to Modern Marketing* (New York: Grand Central Publishing, 2012).

4. "Revenues and Expenditures for Public Elementary and Secondary Education: School Year 2001-02." National Center for Education Statistics. https://nces.ed.gov/pubs2004/rev_exp_02/.

5. "A Nation at Risk." April, 1983. www2.ed.gov/pubs/NatAtRisk/risk.html.

Chapter 2

Getting Started

When working with schools, I often hear the statement, "I just don't know how to get started." Even school administrators who are solidly convinced that marketing is essential to the school's growth and improvement find the process of getting started a major obstacle. Consequently, many good intentions remain just that, intentions.

A good start is essential to a successful marketing effort not only for practical reasons but also for the motivational boost it will give the marketing team. A thorough job in gathering resources, assessing the school's present position, and developing a marketing approach will provide considerable rewards during the implementation, tracking, and future modification of the marketing strategy.

As you begin to design and implement the marketing strategy, an important thing to keep in mind is that you can do as much or as little as you and the marketing team feel comfortable attempting and still achieve some level of positive results. Indeed, a key to success is not taking on more than your resources or capabilities can handle at any one time. A small marketing project successfully completed is preferable to a huge project that fails.

Even if the school already has implemented a marketing initiative, I strongly suggest that the marketing team go through the assessment process described in this chapter. One reason why marketing efforts are not as successful as they could be is that there is no clear and valid assessment of the organization. The result can be decisions based on inaccurate information. Knowing the strengths and weaknesses of your school and the opportunities and threats that influence its success are crucial.

As success leads to greater confidence, the marketing team can attempt strategies that are more complex. If on occasion, efforts do not meet with success, just keep in mind that even the strategies of highly paid marketing experts sometimes fail. Anyone remember the "new" Coca Cola campaign? It was a costly failure by experienced professionals with enviable resources available to them. Mistakes, especially in the beginning, are inevitable. Accept them as lessons and stay motivated.

DEVELOP THE BEST PRODUCT/SERVICE YOU CAN

Providing a quality product or service is the single most important element in any marketing effort. Without a commitment to providing a quality product or service, all marketing efforts are futile. Marketing will not compensate for an inferior educational environment, nor should it.

As stated in the beginning of this book, marketing is not a way to divert attention from a school's deficiencies or its lack of willingness to improve. Build a commitment to excellence into your marketing goals. The information provided in the following pages is designed to help your school create a school that is of value to those the school serves and to promote an awareness of its efforts within the community.

BUILDING A WINNING MARKETING TEAM

Even though I have stated emphatically that everyone in a school has a role in marketing it, a team of motivated individuals is necessary to develop, coordinate, implement, and track the marketing effort. At the school level, the team leader should be the principal or a designated administrator who reports directly to the principal. At the district level, a logical choice for team leader is a marketing, community relations, communication, or public affairs officer who reports directly to the superintendent. It is vital to have a clear understanding that the marketing program is a high-priority activity with the highest level of support.

A team does not need to comprise only school employees. Parents or community members may bring fresh perspectives and useful skills. A middle school I worked with to help with image improvement invited two parents and one of their business partners to be on the team along with the principal, assistant principal, a teacher, and a counselor. Because they were from outside the school environment, these members saw the school through different sets of eyes. Their input was valuable and their enthusiasm and dedication were motivating.

The team leader should have the authority to make routine decisions. If a majority of activities are delayed because someone, not on the team, must review and approve each action, the result will be wasted time, frustration, and loss of momentum.

Initially, the team may be small, comprising a team leader and three or four individuals. Their task is to set preliminary goals and complete a school assessment. Expand the team according to the expected scope of the marketing need. If a major effort is planned, seven to ten members may be needed. To ensure diversity in talent and opinion, I recommend no fewer than four members for any program.

The marketing team will make decisions that have a significant impact on program success, so select members with care. Maximum marketing effectiveness calls for a marketing team whose members possess the following characteristics:

- Belief in the marketing effort. This is the most important qualification. No matter what capabilities a person possesses, if he or she does not believe that the marketing program can make a significant contribution to the school, those capabilities will not be put to best use. True believers will have the dedication to follow through on assignments and remain motivated long term.

  Marketing can be fun and rewarding; however, the work can sometimes be time-consuming and demanding enough to test the commitment of even enthusiastic team members. It is vital that team members believe what they are doing is important, be able to convey that belief to others, and stay motivated even when demands are heavy and results fall short of expectations.
- Willingness to make a long-term commitment. Getting the marketing plan up and running is not something that is likely to happen in a couple of weeks. Team members should be willing to make a commitment for a least several months to a year. A long-term commitment conveys the importance and sincerity of the marketing effort not only to those on the team, but also to individuals or groups with whom the team interacts. If internal and external groups constantly must familiarize themselves with new people and vice versa, the perception is that the effort lacks commitment and organization. Even one or two members dropping out and being replaced can disrupt team spirit and the momentum of activities.
- Good communication skills. Good written and oral communication skills are necessary. This cannot be stressed enough. Good communication is at the heart of your marketing effort. All your marketing activities involve communication in some form.

Some members may be more adept than others at written or oral communication; however, all members should be able to express ideas clearly and concisely, use correct grammar, and construct a logical line of reasoning.

Creative people with technical skills and experience in publishing software and material design are valuable team members.

- Ability to work in a team and independently. Much of the work in the beginning will involve planning and decision-making as a team. Members should be able to develop and sustain a team energy directed at promoting a common vision and shared goals rather than individual projects and objectives. When members pool their work in a coordinated way, the team's efforts are maximized.

However, members often must complete assigned tasks on their own. It is essential that members realize that when they are working independently, they must meet deadlines and complete their assignments as defined by the team. Even one member not contributing his fair share of the work or not meeting deadlines can cause frustration and resentment.

- Willingness to consider another point of view. Being able to look at a problem or issue from all sides is crucial, especially when the school's population is multicultural, there is socioeconomic disparity, or the community is in transition. It may be that negative situations the school now faces are a result of not being aware of other points of view in the community. By welcoming disparate points of view, the marketing team can set the standard for open communication with the school's stakeholders. There may be ideas that, although creative, are simply not possible, especially if there are financial considerations or school policy restrictions that limit what can be done. Therefore, being flexible will keep the program from getting bogged down in a battle of wills.

Issues have multiple sides and there are multiple ways to approach them. Members should be willing to look at all sides, objectively weigh the merits of various ways to proceed, and be willing to support team decisions.

GOALS, OBJECTIVES, AND STRATEGIES

Goals are the results that the school hopes to attain with its marketing efforts. A school may have one or several goals. Goals describe a desired end state. Goals may or may not be achieved totally. Goals may change as situations change.

Goals become actionable when they have measurable objectives attached to them. Objectives are the tasks that must be accomplished collectively for each goal to be reached.

As a goal has objectives attached to it, so an objective will have strategies linked to it. Strategies are the plans that result in actions by which objectives are accomplished and goals are achieved. A strategy is what gets you from where you are to where you want to be.

Think of your marketing effort as analogous to establishing a productive garden. If you were to sow seeds and set plants without any thought as to the purpose of the garden, climate, soil conditions, light, and water requirements, or required maintenance, it is doubtful that you would have much to show for your efforts.

Planting a successful garden requires that you first determine your goal. Is the goal to create a pleasing environment? To provide privacy? To produce food?

The next step is to determine the objectives that will allow you to reach your goal. Objectives might include building the right kind of soil or drawing a layout of the garden.

Finally, your strategy is the overall plan that would include making all possible improvements to your environment, determining the correct time frames for planting, initiating planting stages, and developing methods for maintaining the garden with the proper amounts of fertilizer and water.

Without sufficient attention to all these details, effort and resources are wasted. Not only will you not reap the rewards of fresh and tasty foods or beautiful flowers, you may be discouraged from any future garden projects.

Similarly, the school marketing team should go through a process involving the following steps in Figure 2.1:

When conducting marketing workshops, I am often asked the question, "Shouldn't I assess my school's present situation before I determine what my goals should be?" Well, that depends.

Remember when you and your high school classmates were planning for college? Some of you knew exactly what goal(s) you wanted to accomplish. With these goals in mind, you were able to set out objectives and develop a plan to achieve them based on an assessment of your capabilities and

Determine goals

Assess the school's present position   } May be reversed

Develop marketing plan

Initiate plan

Monitor progress

Figure 2.1   Marketing plan sequence.

resources. Other students needed to assess their capabilities and resources first, and then look at the options available to them. From their set of options, they were better able to set goals.

Similarly, some schools have clear ideas of what they want to accomplish with their marketing programs. Obvious issues, needs, or problems within the school's environment may have created the motivation to initiate a particular marketing program. The marketing team's job is to translate the ideas into understandable, manageable goals and then assess the school's ability to achieve them.

If the marketing team is uncertain about what the school's goals should be, the assessment process described in this section will help them get a clearer picture of areas that need improvement. Goals should reflect those areas of needed improvement.

SMART GOALS

Your marketing team may develop a single or multiple goals. One goal might relate to your volunteer program, another to developing business partners, and another to increasing communication with the community. After goals have been determined, they should be prioritized.

An often-used acronym, *SMART*, is a good tool for developing sustainable goals. *SMART* goals have the following qualities:

- Specific—Goals that are not specific are subject to interpretation. Make your goals as specific as you can. Phrases such as "more effective" or "improved efficiency" have varying interpretations. An individual may consider his efficiency as "improved" if he manages to answer a couple more of his e-mails each day.

   A goal to "improve our volunteer program" is too ambiguous and subjective. "Improve" has different meanings to different people; it may mean one thing to the administration and something else to volunteers. What does *improve* really mean? Does it mean more volunteers? Happier volunteers? Different kinds of volunteers? Who decides when improvement is sufficient?

   If the marketing team is having difficulty forming goals, it may be that they do not understand the related issue well enough. Why does the volunteer program need "improving?" Spend more time determining exactly what the need or problem is, then write a specific goal to correct it.
- Measurable—Goals should be quantifiable. Write goals in a way that allows the team to measure how close the school is to achieving the desired results. A school's goal to "increase interaction with the community" is

stated better as "make one presentation per semester to a local civic organization." If only one presentation is made during the entire school year, you have a measure that indicates that the goal has not been met. Instead of an ambiguous goal to increase volunteer participation, a measurable goal for the volunteer program would be to recruit two volunteers to work with the new music program or to increase the number of reading volunteers from five to eight. Measurable goals eliminate any ambiguity or dispute about how effective efforts are.

- Attainable—It is admirable to set high goals; however, it is not always the best approach when your marketing team is just getting started. Enthusiasm may lead to taking on more than the team can handle. The risk is that the team may fall short of the goals and lose motivation.

To set attainable goals, break big goals into smaller ones. Instead of setting a goal of 100 percent attendance at Parent's Night, figure out what your present attendance is and aim for a 20 percent or 30 percent increase or concentrate on a specific, smaller group such as new parents and aim for a 50 percent increase. Especially in the beginning, success with smaller goals will provide the school with the experience, confidence, and motivation needed to take on larger ones.

Attainable goals are also realistic goals. The definition of marketing speaks to meeting the desires and expectations of the school's various audiences. In setting goals, the team should realize that they cannot meet ALL the desires and expectations of ALL groups or even most. If group A expects one thing that is in direct opposition to what group B expects, the school cannot please both completely.

The marketing team should consider their stakeholders' desires and expectations and make an honest effort to meet them. However, the school's central and most important responsibility is to its students. The desires of individual parents or community members are secondary when they come into conflict with what is best for the students.

- Results oriented—Achievement of the school's goals should lead to the intended results, and there should be an understanding of exactly what those results should be. Frequently goals are created without an understanding of either the desired results or a recognition of possible unintended consequences.

Sometimes administrators tell me one of their goals is to increase the number of volunteers, but when I ask them what they expect the result to be, they are not sure. It sounds like a good idea. However, remember the old adage, "Be careful what you wish for, you might get it." Achieving your goals should not result in additional responsibility that the school is not prepared to handle. If the goal is to increase the number of volunteers, what is the desired result? Is it to lessen the workload of the school staff through volunteer help with office tasks? Will more volunteers achieve that? Or, will training, scheduling, and supervising additional volunteers add to the workload of staff and cause resentment?

The team should ask, if we achieve this goal, what will be the result and will it be advantageous? It is worth spending time to consider the ramification of attaining goals so your success does not lead to unexpected and unwanted circumstances.

• Time related—Without limits, time like money is often wasted. Without time limits, procrastinating is tempting, especially in a school environment where so many other activities are competing for staff time. Setting completion times for projects or activities promotes a sense of importance, holds team members accountable for completing their tasks, and builds satisfaction as projects are accomplished. Do not make timelines so short that everyone is stressed or so long that there is no sense of urgency. You might start out with quarterly, semiannual, and annual goals and adjust as required.

After the team has developed a set of goals, categorize and prioritize them. See if there are links between them so that the team can maximize its efforts. For example, by recruiting volunteers in one area, school staff members and resources can be reallocated to work on improving another area.

At some point, discuss the top two or three goals with other teachers and school staff to solicit suggestions and foster dialogue about how they can participate in achieving them. Remember, everyone is in marketing. Teachers and staff cannot help in the marketing effort unless you inform them about what the effort is supposed to accomplish and provide them guidance about how they can contribute.

KNOW THYSELF

A lack of self-knowledge is a common marketing mistake. People generally feel confident that they are sufficiently knowledgeable about their own organizations. However, this knowledge may be based on unquestioned assumptions, false perceptions, and wishful thinking. Decisions based on inaccurate knowledge lead to mistakes that cost time and money and result in ineffectiveness.

To avoid marketing mistakes based on faulty knowledge, the marketing team should complete a self-assessment process. A systematic, comprehensive way to assess your school's marketing needs is to conduct a SWOT analysis. SWOT stands for Strengths, Weaknesses, Opportunities, and Threats.

The SWOT matrix, shown in Figure 2.2, will help the marketing team assess the school's strengths, weaknesses, opportunities, and threats in five

	Strengths	Weaknesses	Opportunities	Threats
Product				
People				
Price				
Place				
Promotion				

Figure 2.2   SWOT analysis.

areas known as the *5Ps* of marketing: *P*roduct, *P*rice, *P*eople, *P*lace, and *P*ro-motion. Explanations of each of these elements are provided in this chapter.

The purpose of the matrix is to help the marketing team identify school strengths that the school can use in its marketing, pinpoint weaknesses that need to be addressed, determine what threats stand in the way of achieving goals, and find opportunities that can help the marketing effort succeed.

Gather the marketing team and have a white board, chalkboard, or flip chart available. Give team members a copy of the marketing matrix to help them keep focused and organize the information. If you anticipate considerable input for each area, provide a separate sheet for each "P."

As a team, examine each of the five areas looking for strengths, weak-nesses, obstacles, and opportunities. Write comments on the board or chart. Some items may appear in more than one category. For example, students may appear in the people, product, and promotion categories. This exercise often results in comments in one area triggering thoughts for another. Don't constrict your efforts by rigidly trying to fill in one part of the matrix before you move on to another. Just let the comments flow and jump around as needed. When I have participated with a school in this activity, I am amazed at how it brings thoughts and ideas to the surface.

After the first session, team members can spend some time reviewing the matrix, then return for a second session to share new ideas and reach an agree-ment on the school's present position.

In the assessment, include as much information as possible about verifi-able external or community perceptions of the school. External perceptions can provide valuable and often surprising information about your school's perceived strengths and weaknesses and uncover opportunities and threats.

You may be surprised to find that internal perceptions differ from external ones. Major discrepancies in internal and external perceptions signal that the school's judgment of how it is perceived is inaccurate. Address discrepancies in your assessment. If, for example, the administration and staff do not see the physical appearance of the school as a weakness, but information from an external team member reveals that those living around the school find it unattractive, this difference in perception is an issue that should be indicated on the matrix.

The key to using the marketing matrix is to go through the process until the marketing team has a thorough understanding of the school's SWOT. The more information you gather, the more useful your assessment will be.

Keep in mind that as the school's marketing effort moves forward, the assessment will change. As the marketing plan is implemented successfully, strengths are reinforced, weaknesses are diminished or eliminated, opportunities appear, and obstacles are overcome. An annual review of the matrix will provide insight into the success of your marketing efforts.

Completing an assessment is the part of the marketing process that often meets with the most resistance from school administrators. First, administrators and school staff feel that they are sufficiently knowledgeable about their school and its place in the community. Second, the process seems too time-consuming. And, third, it is sometimes hard to convince participants that completing this process now will save time and resources in the future.

I strongly advise *not* to skip this part of the process or to make a cursory attempt. Accurate self-knowledge is essential to sound marketing strategy. The following information provides an explanation of how to complete the matrix.

Strengths are positive attributes that make a school exceptional, different, or advantageous to employees, students, parents, and the community. Obvious strengths are above-average test scores, excellent academic programs, student and teacher awards, exceptional facilities, high graduation rates, and quality extracurricular activities. However, other, less obvious strengths may be overlooked. For example, it speaks well of a school to have dedicated, long-term employees. They are a great strength that should be acknowledged and developed as an asset.

In assessing your strengths, ask questions such as the following:

What are the school's/students'/teachers' achievements?
What do we do exceptionally well?
How are we different in positive ways from other schools?
What special programs do we offer?
Why would someone want to send a child to this school?
Why would a student choose this school over another?
Why would someone want to work or volunteer at this school?

If someone does not have children in a school, why would he support ours? In what ways is the school considered an asset to the community?

Write down every strength you can think of. Put them in the applicable categories. Strengths are the foundation of your marketing program. They are what you have to work with *now.*

We all dislike admitting a weakness, but perfection is rare, so it is best to acknowledge a weakness, then deal with it. In the *Weaknesses* column, be open and truthful. It is counterproductive to justify or ignore deficiencies or to cast the blame on others. If the school's relationship with its immediate neighbors is not good because the residents protest that students are throwing trash around the school, it is not helpful to label the neighbors as whining complainers. This situation signals a weakness in your community relations that needs to be addressed.

Some weaknesses can be turned into an advantage. Avis Rent-A-Car turned their market position as a weak number two to Hertz into a highly successful advertising slogan, "We're Number 2, we try harder." No car manufacturer would view having one of its models labeled a "bug" as a marketing strength. However, Volkswagen produced highly effective and creative ads based on the size and shape of its little car. VWs became cool, fun, and hip, in addition to being inexpensive to buy and economical to operate.

A school might consider it a weakness if it is older than surrounding schools which are newer or more modern looking. If the school, however, has classic architecture, a long presence in the community, a notable list of alumni, or an interesting history, it has advantages the other schools cannot match.

Weaknesses may be in the form of misperceptions about the school that can be corrected through better communication. For example, the school may be having great success with its new reading program, but if most people outside the school do not know about it, the program may not be recognized as one of the school's assets.

After the team has completed the matrix, it should categorize the school's weaknesses. One category should be weaknesses that the school can attend to immediately. For example, the school could address the problem of neighbors who are upset with litter around the school by organizing student clean-up days, adding extra trash receptacles, creating an antilitter campaign, and initiating programs to boost school pride.

In another category, list weaknesses that are most detrimental to the school. Not all of these can be addressed immediately; some may be formidable. Low academic performance, high incidents of student violence, or teacher unrest are serious weaknesses that promote a negative view of the school. Determine what obstacles and opportunities exist that may influence the school's ability to correct these weaknesses.

A third category should include potential weaknesses that need a proactive approach. The potential loss of some of the school's best teachers will lead to a weakness unless action is taken to determine how to retain them. Addressing potential weaknesses can prevent them from becoming a reality.

It may be that much of the initial work in the marketing effort will come from the weakness column; therefore, it is important to give this area considerable attention.

In the *Opportunities* column, try to think of any and every opportunity that could reinforce the school's strengths, remedy its weaknesses, and overcome any threats. In my workshops, this is the column that participants find most difficult. It is sometimes hard to see where opportunities exist. This category requires some imagination.

When looking for opportunities, do not prejudge any possibilities. The tendency is to look for the big event or important person who can have a great impact and save the day. Instead, look upon each person and situation as a possible opportunity.

If you need mentors or volunteers, are there groups in the area that have been overlooked such as the residents of a retirement community? Are there civic organizations that can help with special projects? Are there parents or teachers who can provide referrals to businesses or individuals who have talents the school needs? Is a new residential community being built that could bring in more students? Do school staff or teachers have untapped talents?

While completing the SWOT, a middle school I worked with realized they had a large outdoor area that could be made available to nearby elementary schools. By inviting elementary schools to use its field for sports and community events, the middle school would be creating a marketing opportunity to acquaint potential students and their parents with the school's facilities, programs, teachers, and administrators.

Think about what might be created from existing opportunities. Imagine that a high school's music program has been a source of pride for the school and the students. Teachers credit it with keeping some students in school. However, reduced revenues require that the school reduce funds for the music program. A weakened music program may cause the school to lose students either by transfers to other schools or through dropouts. A staff member mentions that a retirement community has opened recently in the neighborhood. This could be an opportunity.

An effort by the marketing team to recruit volunteers from the retirement community yields a piano teacher who agrees to come one day per week to give piano lessons at a highly reduced rate and a saxophonist who volunteers to work with the students two afternoons a week. Positive interaction with the students and school staff members encourages the saxophonist to recruit two more members from the local music community to volunteer. The musicians persuade a local music store to donate some used instruments. Taking advantage of small opportunities can bring significant benefits that may not be anticipated at first.

Threats are anything that jeopardizes the school's ability to achieve its marketing goals. Competition from other schools or districts can threaten the school's ability to recruit or retain students. A higher pay scale in neighboring districts may threaten the recruitment and retention of highly qualified teachers. A loss of volunteers can threaten the effectiveness of mentoring programs.

In the threats column, list both small and large threats. Small threats may become large if not addressed. Be aware that some threats may be too great to overcome in one effort. However, they may be broken down into smaller hurdles or worn down over time. If an incidence of violence at the school threatens the community's confidence in the school's ability to provide a safe learning environment, time and a range of efforts may be required to restore confidence.

Sometimes we need to go around threats rather than confronting them directly. If the school or district is receiving slanted and unwarranted attacks from a news reporter who refuses to tell a balanced story, it may be necessary to go directly to the public with the school or district's side of the story.

One way to address threats is look in your opportunity list for solutions. One final word on opportunities and threats: opportunities can sneak past you; threats can sneak up on you.

To complete the assessment, assess the strengths, weaknesses, opportunities, and threats of each of the school's 5Ps: Product, People, Price, Place, and Promotion.

For school marketing purposes, *product* refers to any product, service, or attribute that provides benefits for the school's internal or external constituencies. In a school environment, products and services may include students, curricula, extracurricular activities, the school's use as a community center, or its ability to enhance the community's status as a good place to live and work.

Students are the school's most observable products. School strengths are students who meet or exceed standards for moving through successive levels of study, achieve outstanding academic, civic, and community recognition, graduate with the ability to be productive members of the community, or become alumni who contribute to society. Above-average dropout rates, poor student performance, or high levels of truancy are weaknesses. An opportunity might be a grant for a program to decrease the dropout rate. As a product, the school curriculum may have appeal because it is rigorous, specialized, broad, or innovative. Weaknesses include a curriculum that fails to meet the students' needs, for example, a lack of bilingual, college preparatory, or vocational classes. Opportunities include grants to develop new academic programs or improve existing ones. A lack of teachers who can successfully utilize a new curriculum can be a threat to its success.

Extracurricular activities, which enhance the learning experience, such as sports, fine arts activities, debate teams, or school publications are attractive to many students and their parents. To some parents and students these activities are as important as the courses of study. Regard them as a strength of the school. Even for students who do not participate, recognition from these activities can provide a sense of school pride. Poorly administered programs that fail to provide true opportunity for student success are a weakness. Limited resources are often a threat to extracurricular programs. Opportunities may come in the form of alliances with external professional or civic groups that provide extra training or resources for students.

Recognition of the school as a supportive member of the community is an invaluable strength. The services the school provides to the community as a site for civic meetings, election polling, or adult education are an important consideration when assessing the school's services. Assess the quality of interaction with the community. Is the school seen as a reliable partner? Within the limits of its resources, does the school offer services to the community?

Opportunities to reach out to the community are generally plentiful; however, it is important that the school manage external relationships successfully. Detachment or indifference on the part of school administrators and school staff can threaten the perception of the school as one that provides meaningful services to the larger community. If there is a tendency in the school to overlook the general community until a need or crisis prompts greater involvement, then support from the public may be unenthusiastic.

Do not overlook the district's or school's ability to attract people and industry as a valuable service to the community. This attribute is especially important to businesses, government, and civic organizations. Generally, when new families move into a community, the entire community benefits socially and economically. If a principal reason why people move into an area is the school, then it is a valuable asset to the community.

What is your school rating compared to others in your area? Do you have indicators that show one reason people choose or choose not to move to the area is the quality of the schools? The loss of students to other schools in your area is indication of a weakness. Opportunities are occasions to publicize your positive attributes through media sources, presentations, social media, and communication pieces. A threat may be the school's inability or lack of interest in communicating effectively its economic and social benefits to the community.

As the team assesses the products and services the school provides, it should ask the following questions:

- Are our products meeting the needs of our students, their parents, and the community? For example, if many of the students do not intend to go to college, is their education preparing them to compete in the workplace for well-paying jobs? If they are college bound, are students' writing, study, and research skills sufficient?
- What services does the community need that the school could provide, but does not? Could the school provide adult language or driving classes? Is what the school provides the best it can be? Does everyone in the school believe in the school's goals? If not, why not?
- What are the tangible and intangible benefits of the school? Is the school a source of pride within the community?

Critically assess the quality of education your school provides. The marketing effort should involve activities to determine the school's deficiencies and look for ways to improve them. As stated in Chapter 1, no amount of marketing will conceal your school's inability or lack of motivation to provide the best education possible to all children.

The people section includes any person who has or could have an impact on the school.

Students play an important role in the school's assessment. Student achievement, enrollment, satisfaction, and needs should be assessed. Remember, in addition to being products, students are also customers. Their level of satisfaction with courses, teachers, extracurricular activities, and the school environment can be strengths or weaknesses.

The quality of the teachers and school staff the school attracts and retains must be considered. Certainly motivated employees are an asset. If the school has productive, long-term employees, their tenure as employees is a demonstration of loyalty, continuity, and stability that speaks well of the school. Employees are also members of the community and the level of satisfaction, loyalty, and pride they communicate outside the school environment is crucial to how the school is perceived. As customers, their level of satisfaction is influenced by compensation, the work environment, administrative support, and the school's relationship with the community.

Parents and guardians with children in your school can be strengths when they are satisfied, active, and approving of the school's efforts; they can be weaknesses when they are not. Do not ignore people who do not have students enrolled in your school. Do you know who within your community is choosing to instruct their children at home? What is your relationship with them? Home-schooled children may become participants in your extracurricular activities and distance-learning programs or join in school social activities. Their participation provides additional support from their families.

Who are the various groups in your community? Do you know them? Do you know what their needs and expectations of your school are? Is there cultural and language diversity in your community? Is diversity viewed as an obstacle or as an opportunity for the school? Is the community in transition economically or demographically? What is the school's or district's relationship with school board members or other elected officials? How about civic organizations or school-related associations? Are school and district administrators active in such organizations?

A retirement village in your area may be an opportunity for volunteers. Supportive taxpayers are an asset in bond elections. Mutually beneficial relationships with the business owners are crucial in good community relations. What is the school's relationship with these groups?

It is likely that the *People* portion of your assessment will generate the most information. Virtually everyone who is in your community influences your school in some way. However, people offer tremendous opportunity and can be a great asset to the school; therefore, it is advantageous to give as much time and attention as necessary to this section.

In a school environment, the *Place* category refers not only to *where* your product or service is delivered but also *how*. *Where* includes the physical environment of your school such as buildings, grounds, classrooms, equipment, and other facilities. The most obvious example of place is the school structure and grounds.

In assessing place, there are several things to consider. What is the condition of the physical plant and surrounding grounds? Are buildings safe, in good repair, and aesthetically pleasing? Are the grounds attractive? Do classrooms provide sufficient space and the proper equipment for teaching? Is the facility new? Has it been updated? Is it inviting to students, employees, and visitors? What are the security measures? Is it an historic building?

In the case of one elementary school in a major city, two characteristics of place helped the school develop a beneficial relationship within the community. The unique characteristics that set it apart from other schools in the district were its place in history and its architecture. The school is the oldest continuously occupied school in the district. Its classic Spanish-style architecture embraces the playground with old world grace. A serendipitous meeting between the principal and a local resident, who stopped by one day to see the building, began a successful relationship with the local civic association that has helped form a bond between the school and the community.

The local civic association saw the classic architecture of the school as an asset that could benefit property values by helping to maintain the character of the neighborhood. Residents who wanted to preserve the old building established a nonprofit organization specifically to raise money for the school.

When the school district made plans to renovate the school, administrators recognized the importance of place in the school's relationship with the community. The decision was to preserve the architectural style. Previous temporary additions to the original building, which were not in keeping with the Spanish style, were removed and replaced with new space in the original architectural style.

Because of its history and architecture, the school is on the civic association's annual home tour and many alumni return for a visit during that time. Twice each year—once right before the home tour—the school holds Gardening Day. Parents, students, and residents put in new plants, trim bushes, and pull weeds around the school. Recognition of place has provided the school with new and continued community support.

The *how* aspect of *place* includes how your product is delivered. For example, teaching methodologies, whether traditional or innovative, may be an asset or a weakness. If a new approach to teaching math produces outstanding results, it is a strength. Obviously, methods that are not producing the desired results are a weakness.

The use of technology to deliver instruction and remedial support is increasingly important to parents, teachers, and the community. An aggressive plan that brings needed technology into the school is a strength. A lack of basic or up-to-date technology is a weakness the school can address through opportunities provided by federal programs and relationships with external organizations.

How students access educational services is included in place. Weaknesses exist when it is difficult or time-consuming for students to get to school or if parents are reluctant to put their children on a school bus because the safety record is poor, bus breakdowns are frequent, or the pick-up and drop-off places are unsafe. Threats may be a lack of funds to replace old equipment or the inability to hire and retain qualified bus drivers.

Price is an obvious consideration for private schools. Parents should feel their children are receiving an education that justifies the tuition and fees they pay. A cost-benefit ratio weights the cost against the quantitative and qualitative benefits derived. Private schools generally are more aware of the cost-benefit ratio than public schools. They must generate sufficient revenue to continue to provide the quality of education parents want for their children, but still remain affordable for their target market. Virtually all private schools also factor in costs of scholarships which allow them to provide a more inclusive learning environment.

It should be recognized that free public education is not really free. Virtually every adult supports public education directly or indirectly through taxes and school bonds. One of the greatest strengths of public schools is the quality education they offer for the dollars expended per student. When compared with some private schools, public schools may provide a level of education excellence that is equal to or greater at a smaller cost. However, it is also true that public schools may fall short of meeting this standard. When community members examine public education as taxpayers, they also use the cost-benefit approach. Consideration of this comparison should be a part of any marketing effort. A major strength for a public school is recognition that the school's or district's benefit to the community is equal to or greater than the cost.

Increasingly high costs of salaries for quality teachers, technology, and maintenance and construction of buildings are challenges every school faces. For public schools, these challenges are compounded by taxpayers who are opposed to increasing revenue through higher taxes and school bonds. Marketing is important in tax increases and bond referendums. Often a lack of support for additional revenue sources is based on inadequate information. If the public does not understand the issues that require additional funding, they cannot make informed decisions. For example, many taxpayers are not aware of how schools are funded.

When a bond referendum for a large urban school district failed to pass, research after the fact showed that many people did not understand how public schools were funded and why the district needed additional revenue. It was determined that these misunderstandings were largely responsible for the failure. The district created a brochure that explained exactly how tax dollars flow from tax payers to school districts and made a concerted effort to explain to the community specifically how the district would use the bond money. The next bond referendum passed.

Costs are not always monetary. Time and effort provided by volunteers, parents, business partners, and civic groups have great value to the school and should be included in the price assessment. Strong community participation is one of a school's greatest strengths. Apathy, alienation, and competing demands may be threats. If so, give them special attention in your marketing plan.

Opportunities in the price section come from new people and businesses in your community, grants and financial assistance, and a growing awareness of the contribution your school makes to the community. It should be the goal of your marketing effort to make the most of these opportunities.

Promotion includes any activities and materials the school uses to reach out to its various stakeholders, build a caring internal environment, and create an awareness of the school's efforts to meet the public's desires and expectations. Promotional activities should support and enhance your marketing goals.

In assessing your promotion section, first look at what you are doing or have done that was successful. Is your website generating positive feedback?

Did your school open house generate interest in your school? Have you formed beneficial business alliances? Did your volunteer recruitment campaign succeed? Discuss all your promotional activities and review your marketing materials.

Under Strengths, list materials and activities that met their objectives and determine why they were successful. Under Weaknesses, list those that have not succeeded and try to determine why they failed. Do not personalize any failures. It may be that good ideas were implemented at the wrong time or without sufficient planning or resources. Sometimes good strategies are abandoned because time frames were unrealistic. Given more time, they may have succeeded.

Threats are as varied as the activities. Does your promotional effort lack support from the top administrators? Your school board? Do you feel that you do not have sufficient internal staff to plan and carry out effective activities? Do you need external expertise, but feel that you cannot afford it? Are there linguistic and cultural obstacles that must be overcome?

In the beginning of your marketing effort, keep doing the things that are working and choose new activities that are within the range of the school's resources and expertise. However, take care not to become complacent. A communication piece that was successful may have become outdated and need to be revised. Find additional activities the school can use to improve relationships with internal and external groups.

WHO IS YOUR COMPETITION?

After the marketing team has completed the school's assessment, it should determine who the school's competitors are and assess them using the same matrix. Competition may not come solely from another school or district but also from apathy within or separation from the community. Competition must be addressed if you are to reach your goals.

Information about competitors may be limited, but the team should gather as much data as it can. An awareness of the strengths and weaknesses of the school's competition is an essential part of developing an effective strategy to position it as a desirable choice for students and as an asset to the community.

BEING DIFFERENT MAKES A DIFFERENCE

Why do consumers select one product over another? Because one product offers something to the consumer that the others do not. That "something" could be price, special features, ease of use, status, name recognition, or any number of things that appeal to the consumer. Parents and students select a school for a reason, even if the reason is simply that it is in the neighborhood or it is the school their friends chose. Whatever the reason, the school offered something another school did not.

Because administrators and teachers tend to see themselves as doing the same kinds of things in parallel ways with similar goals, defining what makes their school different is often difficult. Use the Assessment Matrix to help determine what sets your school apart from other schools. Do you have a long-standing presence in the community? (Place). Are you in a historic building? (Place). Are you in a new, high-tech building? (Place). Do you have bilingual, arts, sciences, reading, or extracurricular programs that are above average or have gained recognition? (Product). Are your support organizations such as the PTO, booster clubs, volunteers, and businesses especially strong? (People). Do you offer a special cultural or religious environment? (Place). Do you offer a desirable teaching methodology? (Product) What are the special achievements of your students? (Product, People). Your teachers? (People). Are school employees active in community activities? (People, Promotion). The marketing team should ask the question, "What makes our school special?," and then answer in as many ways as they can.

TAKE A POSITION

The school's positioning statement is not the same as the school's position. The school has a position whether it markets itself or not. The school's position is how it is perceived by its various internal and external groups. The school may do things to influence its position, but it is created in the minds of its audiences.

The positioning statement, however, is a one or two sentence statement that defines how the school *wants* its various audiences to perceive it. It is the core message that the school wants to send to its constituencies. It defines for internal and external audiences who you are, what you offer, to whom you offer it, and why you are different. It is the sum of the school's attributes. It articulates why the school is distinctive.

If you have completed the SWOT and objectively assessed your 5 Ps, you should have a good understanding of your position with its strengths, weaknesses, opportunities, and threats. Now the marketing team should use information from the SWOT matrix to write a positioning statement. The statement is not something that is written in a 30-minute meeting. It takes time and thought. Seek input from internal and external groups to help develop it. Expect revisions as the team refines the statement. The positioning statement should answer the following questions with a succinct, strong statement:

Who are we?

How does the school define itself? Is the school a magnet school, Montessori school, exemplary school, established neighborhood school?

What does our school offer?

Does it offer special language, technical, or college preparatory curriculum? A caring environment? An accelerated curriculum? Fine arts programs? A rigorous science and math curriculum? A faith-influenced environment?

What are the benefits of what we offer?

How does what the school offers benefit its various constituencies?

How is our school different?

Does the school have innovative programs, above-average achievement scores, a highly qualified teaching staff, a special academic ranking, a wide range of extracurricular activities, an attractive campus, small class sizes, special facilities, special community involvement, or other attributes that make your school different from other schools? Differentiation is a key element in your positioning statement. It is the part of your positioning statement that says, "This is how we are different from others."

Do not fall into the trap of creating a positioning statement that the school cannot support. Be realistic. If the difference between your position and your position statement is too great, your audiences will not accept it. The ultimate goal is for the school's position to align with its positioning statement, that is to say, that the internal and external audiences perceive the school as it wants to be perceived. Create a statement that makes that possible.

Often positioning statements do not receive the attention they deserve. A well-written positioning statement provides the direction and focus the marketing team needs to develop and adhere to the marketing plan now and in the future.

Positioning statements relate to the present, but the school also needs a mission that relates to the future and provides motivation for continued improvement.

WHAT'S YOUR MISSION?

In the early 1960s, President John Kennedy set for the United States the mission of putting an American on the moon and returning him safely within the decade. It was a bold mission that inspired a courageous, focused, and ultimately successful effort to put the United States in the forefront of space exploration.

Frequently, I see mission statements that resemble advertising slogans more than a statement of purpose. If an airline tells me its mission is to make me a "happy repeat flyer," I am inclined to see this as promotion. A more believable, if not as catchy, statement might be, "To earn our place as a major international carrier by creating innovative incentive programs, in-flight attention, and pre- and post-flight services designed to meet the needs of business and leisure travelers." Wouldn't that be nice!

A mission or vision gives the school a future goal to target. It is the moon the school wants to shoot for. The purpose is to provide a focus for forward movement. Be bold in your mission statement. Ask, "What could we really do if we put our hearts and minds into it?" A statement without passion will provide lackluster results.

Harry Beckwith states that if a mission statement is well written, most employees can regularly answer the question, "What have you done this week to advance the mission?" From time to time, ask administrative and office staff, teachers, and other employees what they have done recently to support the school's or district's mission. If more than a few cannot give you an answer, then the mission statement is not having the desired effect.

WORDS TO LIVE BY

Often positioning and mission statements are created to help get the marketing effort organized, but then forgotten until the program loses focus and momentum. Do not let the school's positioning and mission statements become catchphrases that sound good but have little meaning or effort behind them. Use them to keep your marketing effort on track.

Periodically, begin marketing team meetings by reviewing the positioning and mission statements and discussing what is being done to fulfill them. Use them to guide communication and public relations activities. Recognize accomplishments that reflect the school's mission and display them in places where employees, students, and parents can see them. If you find that the school's mission is not providing the focus and motivation for which it was created, revise it.

ALWAYS HAVE A PLAN

As stated earlier, marketing strategy is what gets the school from where it is to where it wants to be. The assessment process has helped the marketing team determine where the school is. The positioning and mission statements provide direction. Now, the strategy is to make the most of the school's strengths, improve weaknesses, address threats, and take advantage of opportunities to take it where it wants to go.

After the marketing team has completed the assessment, written a positioning statement, and determined its mission, it is ready to articulate the marketing strategy through a plan. A marketing plan is exactly that, a plan for how to achieve marketing goals. The purpose is to keep the marketing effort focused and on schedule.

Opinions vary on what a plan should include and how long it should be. I once read an article in which a marketing guru said that a plan should fit on a cocktail napkin. Others will argue that a plan of any worth would fill a dozen pages. Of course, some corporate marketing plans may be complex. This is especially true when companies are launching a new product and the marketing plan includes market research, market-segment profiles, revenue projections, and production schedules. However, the school's marketing team should be able to construct an initial marketing plan in no more than a few pages.

The school's initial marketing plan provides an overview of the marketing strategy: What does the school hope to accomplish within what time frame and with what resources? As the marketing efforts progress, expand the plan to include more details. Anything more than several pages should be divided into an overall marketing plan and smaller project plans. The plan should provide the marketing team with an outline of what it hopes to accomplish within a specific time frame.

The following case study is provided to give you a better understanding of the assessment process, positioning and mission statements, and the marketing plan.

A CASE STUDY

Riverside High School

Riverside High School is located in a close-in neighborhood within a large metropolitan area. The school was built in the early 1950s when the community comprised mostly middle-class working people. Over time, the neighborhood has changed to one that is more racially mixed and economically diverse with a large number of retired people. In addition to public schools, several parochial elementary and middle schools are located in the area, but there is no other high school nearby.

In the last couple of years, large tracts of land became available when some abandoned manufacturing plants were demolished and the land was cleared. Developers bought these tracts to meet the growing demand for new close-in housing and are building moderate to expensive single-family dwellings, low-rise apartments, townhouses, and some commercial construction. Plans are to complete 300 new residences within Riverside's boundaries within the next three to five years. Local realtors estimate that 40 percent of these residences will have occupants with school-age children. It is likely that the new residents will comprise middle- to high-income professionals and some well-off retired people.

Over the last five years, under the leadership of its principal, Mr. Johnston, Riverside High School achieved "recognized" status, the second highest ranking given by the state accreditation agency. The new academic rating has raised student and teacher morale and generated praise from the community. As a result of the new ranking and the work of teachers and administrative staff members, the school has received a $200,000, two-year grant from a local chemical corporation to start a "Scientists in the Making" program. However, some of the school's most experienced and popular teachers, who were instrumental in Riverside's academic improvement, may soon retire.

The PTO has gained new members and become more proactive. Recently their fund-raising activities generated enough money to install new landscaping. The members have also worked closely with school administrators and parents to address school safety issues.

Riverside has a strong vocational education program that offers classes in auto mechanics, culinary arts, and technology-related subjects. Equipment for these classes is becoming obsolete. The school has dedicated money to update the equipment for vocational education, but the gymnasium is also in need of renovation.

Employee relations are good, but some teachers have begun to complain lately that too much money is spent on sports. Their complaints have caused some difficulties in gathering support for renovations to the gymnasium. The school district's Board of Education is considering allowing naming rights in return for renovation funds. Some parents and teachers find this option offensive and oppose the idea.

The school's relationship with the community has always been good. The local paper has been helpful in promoting the school to the community. Several established businesses, including local realtors, have actively supported the school over the years. However, the business environment is changing to meet the new demographics. New businesses are expected to move into the area to serve the expanding and more diverse population.

At the beginning of the next school year, Academy for Academic Excellence (AAE), a for-profit school, will open. Initially, the school will offer classes from pre-K through grade 8; but AAE plans to add a high school within the next several years. AAE has an aggressive and well-funded marketing effort. The school is positioning itself as a forward-thinking organization that provides a classic education in a high-tech environment. In the past few months, AAE's director of marketing has made presentations to two local civic associations.

Riverside wants to develop a marketing program that will capture a substantial portion of the new residential market and position itself to face any competition from AAE, while continuing to meet the needs of the community of which it has been a part for so many years. The marketing effort is meeting with some resistance from school staff members who see it as just more work.

Now look at the Assessment Matrix in Figure 2.3 for an example of responses that a marketing team might have included in an assessment of Riverside High School. Although this is not an in-depth assessment, it will give you an idea of how the marketing team might begin a matrix. Even with the limited amount of information in the matrix, the marketing team can determine that despite the school's significant strengths, a concerted marketing effort is needed to address the possible loss of key teachers, growing internal tension, and highly organized competition that could erode their present and future enrollment.

The marketing team has decided that the high school should position itself as a school that has achieved success through attributes that benefit all the students and that the intent is to continue to maximize student potential. The team feels it is also important to recognize that the school has always enjoyed good community support, but that the community is changing and

	Strengths	Weaknesses	Opportunities	Threats
Product	Scientists in the Making Program. Vocational Ed. AP program next year Recognized Status	Needs funds to sustain and expand curriculum	Possibility of expanding science program if more funds become available	Possible retirement of some teachers could affect the science program
People	Excellent teachers. Active PTO. Good leadership & employee relations. High student morale. Key communicators	Not all staff members support marketing effort. Need external marketing expertise	Additional students from new housing addition. More PTO members	Discontent of some employees regarding new initiatives
Price	Community support. Grant money	Need to be more proactive in pursuing additional funds.	Possibility of additional grant money and support from businesses if science program is successful	New for-profit school could take present and future students from us
Place	New science equipment & materials. PTO provided new landscaping.	Gym in need of repair	School board may approve selling advertising space to bring in funds for gym repair.	Resistance to advertising to raise money for gym
Promotion	Good relationships with local businesses. Positive media coverage of science program.	Need more, better organized promotional activities	Some business partners have agreed to help with marketing activities	New for-profit school has well organized and funded marketing campaign. They have already contacted some of our local businesses and orgs.

Figure 2.3   Riverside High School Assessment Matrix

the school will respond to those changes. Below is an example of a positioning statement that would reflect this way of thinking.

RIVERSIDE HIGH SCHOOL POSITIONING STATEMENT

*Riverside High School is a Recognized school proud of its success in creating
an environment in which every student benefits from high standards, innovative programs, a dedicated teaching staff, and a safe environment. We are
dedicated to preserving the strong community support we enjoy by continuing
to meet the education needs of our changing, diverse neighborhood.*

Let's take a look at this statement. Riverside High School positions itself as
an organization of significant accomplishment through awareness of its new
status as a recognized school and its success in providing the means for student
achievement. It states what it offers to those who attend the school and recognizes that the school is there to serve *all* its students. This recognizes that with
changing demographics, students' needs may also be changing and the school
will meet those needs. The statement concludes by reinforcing the importance
of community support and the school's intention of maintaining that support by
being flexible enough to serve a changing community. Riverside is positioning
itself as a school of achievement that will continue to meet the needs of the
community that has supported it for decades while adapting to the community's
changing demographics. It is a message of dedication, assurance, and progress.
   Riverside's achievements in the past few years have raised school morale
and expectations. The marketing team wants to create a mission that will
motivate continued improvement.

RIVERSIDE HIGH SCHOOL MISSION

*Our goal is to capitalize on the talents and dedication within our school and
community to achieve the highest school ranking of Exemplary within the next
three years.*

This is an unambiguous statement of a high, but achievable mission. It affirms
that the school has the internal and external means to achieve its mission
within a stated time frame. This is a mission that leaves no doubt about what
the school wants to accomplish. This statement makes it possible for administrators, teachers, staff members, students, parents, and external audiences to
ask themselves and each other at any time, "What are we doing to achieve our
mission?" and from their answers be able to determine their progress.

RIVERSIDE HIGH SCHOOL MARKETING PLAN

After much work, the Riverside marketing team is now ready to create an initial marketing plan. The initial plan is a framework upon which to build. The team can expand and refine it as necessary. As ideas are generated and activities are initiated, the plan will include more detail. The plan begins with the positioning statement, mission, and goals and a summary of the SWOT to keep the team focused and avoid plan "creep," the tendency to move in a direction or expand the plan in a way that is not consistent with the intent of the marketing effort. The Potential Market and Competition reinforce the present opportunity and the threat. These parts of the marketing plan are not likely to change in the near future.

The remainder of the plan will undergo the most revision. A timeline for the year with activities will likely be expanded and revised after the marketing initiative is launched. Some of the activities may develop into separate plans with designated teams. The resources needed may change as activities are expanded or modified. Noting the names of the team members is recognition of each member's commitment. Finally, the benefits are stated to keep the team motivated.

MARKETING PLAN—RIVERSIDE HIGH SCHOOL

Positioning Statement

Riverside High School is a Recognized school that is proud of its success in creating an environment in which *every* student benefits from high standards, innovative programs, a dedicated teaching staff, and a safe environment. We are dedicated to preserving the strong community support we enjoy by continuing to meet the education needs of our changing, diverse neighborhood.

Mission

Our goal is to capitalize on the talents and dedication within our school and community to achieve the highest school ranking of Exemplary within the next five years.

Goals

To increase academic achievement in all core subjects
To maintain all current external partnerships
To add three new partnerships among the new businesses in our area

To have a minimum of one positive news story each month in the local paper
To make one presentation each school year to each of the civic associations
in our area
To create new marketing materials
To update the school website and develop social media channels
To capture 60 percent of the potential high school students among new home-
owners within the next five years.

SWOT

Strengths: School achieved "Recognized" rating last two years. $200,000,
two-year grant from XYZ Corporation for "Scientists in the Making"
Program. Highly qualified, dedicated teachers. Good leadership. Proactive
PTA/PTO organization. Good community support

Weaknesses: Support for marketing effort is not strong enough. Gym needs renovation. Vocational classes need better equipment. Inadequate funds to implement all needed improvements. Few AP and college preparatory classes.

Opportunities: New residential and commercial construction in the area.
Three major realty companies have indicated a willingness to participate in
our marketing effort, local newspaper is very supportive of public schools,
increasing population with greater diversity. New technology person familiar with social media strategies.

Threats: New K-8, for-profit school with a significant marketing campaign is
opening next fall within our school boundaries. Opposition to gym renovations.
Discontent among staff over new initiatives. Possible retirement of teachers.

Potential Market

Potential for additional student from new development in the area. Realtors
estimate that within our school's boundaries 300 new residences will be
completed within the next 3–5 years. Past sales indicate that 40 percent of
these homes will have occupants with school-aged children.
Potential for increased external support from new commercial development
in the area
Potential to lose present students if shift to accommodate the wants and expectations of new students is perceived as abandonment of current student body

Competition

In the fall of 2005, Academy for Academic Excellence (AAE), a for-profit
school, will open. AAE has an aggressive and well-funded marketing effort.
They are positioning themselves as an organization that provides a classic
education in a high-tech environment.

Activities/Timeline

Sep–Oct: Set up marketing team schedule, add members to team, and assign tasks
Determine need for research and initiate as required
Determine marketing audiences and develop appropriate messages and activities
Hold brainstorming sessions as needed
Develop public relations ideas
Create and pretest marketing materials
Establish contacts with external partners
Begin to build a database
Begin making changes to website and initiate social media channels
Set up teams to work on "weaknesses"
Meet with fund-raising committee to coordinate efforts for gym renovation
Develop a presentation for external audiences

Nov: Produce marketing materials
Acquaint all internal staff, students, and external partners with new marketing materials and initiatives
Implement marketing effort

Dec: Set up tentative presentation schedule for remainder of school year

Jan–Feb: Monitor marketing efforts and make adjustments as required
Reaffirm relations with present external partners and reach out to new ones
Initiate public relations ideas as resources permit
Evaluate efforts to improve weaknesses

Mar–Apr: Develop next year's marketing and public relations program based on analysis of present marketing efforts
Conduct surveys to aid marketing efforts

May: End-of-school event, build enthusiasm for next school year
Set up plan so that marketing efforts are maintained during the summer

Jun–Aug: Maintain marketing effort as time and resources allow

Required Resources

Manpower: *First three months*—3–5 hours per person per week for internal team members, 1–2 hours per week for support staff, 1–2 hours per person per week for external members.

Remaining months—1–2 hours per week for team members, 1–2 hours per week for support staff, 0–2 hours per week for external members.

Money: $2000–$5000
Materials: Marketing materials and presentation
Machines: Copying equipment, digital camera
Methods: Marketing—Public relations—Customer service—Advertising

Marketing Team

Robert Johnston, Principal
Ellen Grunell, Assistant Principal
Allen Archer, Business Manager
Alicia Cooper, Teacher
Belinda Gardner, Hudson Realty

Benefits

Increase new student population
Retain present student population
Build new relationships with the external partners
Facilitate needed improvements
Attract and retain highly qualified staff
Enhance standing in the community
Systematic plan for improved marketing and public relations

LEVERAGE YOUR BRAIN POWER

"Two heads are better than one" is a core belief of brainstorming.

Effective brainstorming sessions can foster creative thinking and produce imaginative solutions. Thoughts produce ideas that generate discussion that stimulates thinking that leads to more ideas. If the sessions are focused, the atmosphere is motivating, and free thinking and expression are encouraged, creativity and innovation will result.

Too often, however, brainstorming sessions produce the same old ideas reconstituted or lapse into a litany of grievances and complaints. Following a few simple guidelines can make your sessions a worthwhile activity.

- Create the right environment. If possible, conduct the session away from the school in a comfortable, relaxed environment that encourages inventive thinking. If a site away from school is not an option, make the session room as visually pleasant as possible with flowers, plants, or visually appealing posters (with themes or images unrelated to school). Chairs should be comfortable and arranged informally. Set aside a minimum of two hours time. If possible, schedule early in the day when minds are less likely to be overtaxed from daily activities.

Large projects, such as planning a community parade and fair, may require multiple sessions. Provide a selection of beverages and light snacks. If the session is long enough to include lunch, keep it simple. Have at least one easel with a full pad of paper, colored pens, and tape or pins to stick sheets on the wall. Provide each participant with plenty of paper, index cards, colored pens, even creative toys. Include idea provokers related to the purpose of the session such as sample brochures, magazines, layout or design books, newspaper articles, case studies, short stories, videos, or photographs.

- Start with a clear statement of purpose and stick to it. Write one clear, specific statement that defines exactly what is to be accomplished. Write it large and place it on an easel or tape it on the wall so that everyone can see it during the session.

  Examples of statements of purpose:

  "To generate ideas for our new fine arts program brochure that will encourage more minority students to become involved"

  "To determine the theme of our school float in the annual neighborhood parade and how we should illustrate the theme"

  "To find three new ways we can increase participation of new immigrant parents in our school"

  "To generate ideas for making our new teacher luncheon motivational for both new and experienced teachers"

  "To find ways to generate greater participation from our business partners in the Back to School event"

  Do not let the session wander offtrack. If new issues arise, write them down for future consideration, but keep focused on your present objectives.

- Select the right participants. Select people who are creative and outgoing, but also include methodical, analytical thinkers. They are the ones who figure out how to make creative ideas a reality. Avoid chronic naysayers or people who are likely to dominate the session and inhibit participants from freely expressing themselves.

  Aim for diversity. It is a good idea to pick some people who are familiar with the issue or project and some who are not. Include people with different functions and different talents. If possible, include people who are representative of your target audience, such as students, volunteers, or business partners. Include enough people to achieve some diversity, but do not exceed seven or eight people.

Designate a session leader to coordinate the preparations and lead the activities. Send a notice at least a week in advance. In addition to time and place, the notice should provide participants with a brief overview that includes the purpose of the session and any background material that might help participants prepare for it. Encourage participants to think about the session topic and collect materials they think may be helpful in stimulating ideas and discussion. There are some of us who need to think quietly before we experience the great "Aha!"

• Conduct a productive session. The session leader should start by welcoming the participants and thanking them for their time. Give a brief overview; then, allow time for questions. Hand out a copy of the session rules and guidelines or post an enlarged copy on the wall next to the objective. Discuss each one before the session starts to reinforce them. Following are some rules and guidelines to consider:

Turn off cell phones
Indulge in atypical thinking
Avoid negativity. Don't look for what is wrong with an idea, look for what is right
Remember there is no such thing as a dumb idea. An idea that doesn't work today may work tomorrow
Let one idea lead to another
Take an idea and run with it.

It is up to the leader to ensure that the session stays on task and that everyone is participating. Make an effort to include those who may be reluctant to participate and to keep in check those who may try to dominate the session. If enthusiasm wanes or creative block sets in, engage in a brief physical activity, then stop for a couple of minutes of meditation or quite time or play a creative game or puzzle.

It is helpful to have an assistant to the leader (not one of the session participants) write ideas on the easel pad as they are generated and stick them on the wall, assist with any creative games, and help with lunch and refreshments.

At least once during the session, twice if the session is long, stop to review the ideas. Vote on the ones to keep. Think of ways to improve or build upon the ideas you keep. Then start on a new set of ideas.

Take a 10-minute break after 50 minutes.

About half an hour before the session ends rank the ideas. Take the best ideas and try to improve them. Be sure to keep all the notes and flip chart pages. Some of the ideas not selected may be useful at another time.

At the end of the session, assign "next steps" to the appropriate people.

In some cases, the group may not feel the session has been sufficiently productive. In this case, the participants should write down the ideas generated then leave and let their subconscious minds do the work. A week later, meet again. The chances are good that the result will be a more productive session.

- Encourage ideas. Marketing thrives on creativity. Creativity requires a willingness to express ideas that others may consider controversial, silly, nontraditional, and even wacky. It is up to the team leader to establish an environment in which participants feel free to express ideas without fear of censure or ridicule.

Be aware of and give consideration to shyness or cultural traditions that may inhibit the kind of nonconforming thinking and self-expression looked for in a creative brainstorming session. To overcome participant shyness or cultural reticence, use silent brainstorming. Give each participant several large index cards at the beginning of the session. Participants can write down any ideas or comments they have. Ask every participant to write down at least one idea. The cards can be dropped into a box or collected at a break toward the end of the session. On a flip chart, write the ideas large enough for everyone to see them. Tear the sheets off and tape them on the wall. When the participants return from their break, go through the ideas one by one. Check those the team wants to pursue further.

- Follow up after the session. Send each participant a thank you memo with a summary of session accomplishments and subsequent action. Follow up with any participants who were assigned tasks for progress reports.

At this point, the marketing team should have sufficient understanding of the school's strengths, weaknesses, opportunities, and threats and established goals based on that understanding. With a positioning statement, a mission, a marketing plan, and some ideas, the team is now ready to move forward with the marketing initiative.

Chapter 3

Marketing Research and Database Marketing

For decades marketing professionals have conducted research to determine customer needs, wants, and satisfaction levels, pretest new products, and forecast trends. The benefits of "opinion" research led to its use by political and advocacy groups. Things happen. Perceptions vary. Demographics shift. Opinions evolve. Keeping abreast of change requires continual investigation.

Don't let the term "marketing research" intimidate you. Marketing research involves any activity that provides the information you need to make informed marketing decisions. Marketing research can take a variety of forms. It can be an informal chat with members at a civic club luncheon about the upcoming school initiative or a professionally conducted community survey concerning multiple issues. Actually, marketing research is not much different from research conducted for other purposes such as determining political or economic environments. The difference is that marketing research is focused on gathering information specifically to guide marketing activities.

A key to productive research is a genuine desire to obtain the information needed to make better decisions. Research as window dressing to imply interest in constituencies' opinions or to bolster decisions already made is a waste of resources. The research methods described in this section should help the school either conduct a useful research project itself or, if someone else is conducting the research, to know what they should be doing.

WHO ARE YOUR CONSTITUENCIES AND
WHAT ARE THEY THINKING?

Rarely will people make an appointment for a meeting to tell you why they are not sending their children to your school. Potential business partners will not call to discuss the reasons why they are not working with your school. New residents will not call to tell you that they have moved into the neighborhood so you can update your demographic information. Parents will not come to a school event to offer their rationale for not participating in school activities. However, this is information schools need to determine their marketing goals, assess the school's present position, and make sound marketing decisions. Decisions based on assumptions and partial knowledge result in a waste of resources, poor relations with internal and external groups, and a loss of better educational opportunities for students.

Knowing why some parents or students do not select your school as their education choice is as important as knowing why some do. Parents who have chosen not to enroll their children in your school can provide valuable insight into how the community perceives your school. Ask parents and students what influenced their choices. What did your school offer that others did not? Or, if they chose another school, why? Did they consider your school at all? Did they visit the school? What were their impressions? What, if anything, would influence a decision to reconsider your school?

Today, finding out who your constituencies are and what they think are necessary activities for any school that wishes to build support and credibility with internal and external groups. How do schools find out these things? One of the best ways—sometimes the only way—is to ask.

School administrators often neglect marketing research because they view it as a complicated, expensive, and time-consuming endeavor. Others see marketing research as unnecessary because they feel that they truly know and understand what internal and external groups think about them. A few are afraid that negative responses will result in harmful publicity. And the worst reason of all—it may require that they address an issue they would rather avoid. When persuaded, however, to conduct a community, employee, or student survey, administrators find the data often show surprising results. The steps in any market research process are:

1. Determine your research objectives
2. Develop a research plan
3. Collect the data
4. Analyze the collected data; and
5. Take action on the results.

Conducting some level of marketing research on a regular schedule provides valuable information that helps schools stay abreast of changes in their internal and external environments, communicate more effectively with internal and external groups, determine public perceptions, meet community expectations, increase levels of employee and student satisfaction, and build support for school or district initiatives.

SETTING RESEARCH OBJECTIVES

Before beginning any type of research, it is important to have a clear understanding of what the school hopes to achieve by gathering information. If the survey targets parents and students to determine their needs, desires, and expectations, what does the school intend to do with the information it gathers? If the study shows that many students and parents want accelerated classes, is the school prepared to make changes to the curriculum? Or add special courses? If a survey of volunteers shows that they are leaving because of apathy and disorganization within the school, is the school willing to address their grievances with action?

To help establish marketing research objectives, think carefully about what information the school needs to move forward with its marketing efforts or even what those efforts should be. A question to ask is: What do we already know and how do we know it? The key word here is *know*, not assume. The school cannot know the level of parent approval, employee satisfaction, or community support without periodically checking the validity of its information. Having determined what the school does know, the marketing team can then determine what additional information it needs to gather.

Below are examples of school- or district-related research issues:

Who in the community does not send their children to our school and why?
How much does the community actually know about the school or district?
How does the community get information about the school or district?
What level of credibility does the school have within the community?
What are the perceptions held by various groups within the community relating to specific topics (school safety, communication, the school board, the administration)?
What is the status of parent/teacher relations?
Who are the school's competitors and why are they competitive?
What are the top five concerns of the students? Of parents? Of employers?
What is the level of volunteer satisfaction? Employee satisfaction? Student satisfaction?

Once you have established your objectives, the next step is to decide how to gather the information you need. The following paragraphs describe the commonly used means to gather information including literature searches, surveys, focus groups, and interviews. Each method has advantages and disadvantages.

WHAT YOU NEED MAY BE A CLICK AWAY

There is no reason to collect the information you need if someone already has it. Information may be readily available from sources such as government or nonprofit agencies, the Internet, universities, or published research papers. Information about the demographics of your community is available from city, county, or national census data. A local university may have conducted studies regarding local public opinion on issues related to education. Information about businesses in your area is available through company websites or the archives of local newspapers.

A wealth of information is available via the Internet. Newspapers, magazines, trade publications, academic journals, government data at the federal, state, and local levels, and websites of your competition, similar types of schools, and businesses may provide some of the information you need. One of the fastest ways to find sources of information is through Internet search engines. When you find a particularly useful source, add the link to your "Favorites" list so you can call it up easily.

A literature search is an inexpensive way to gather information; however, bear in mind that the information may not be as up-to-date as you need. Moreover, a literature search will not provide you with specific information regarding the opinions and perceptions of your internal and external audiences. The best way to gather that kind of information is through contact with the people in those groups. The school can accomplish that through interviews, focus groups, and surveys.

USE INTERVIEWS AND FOCUS GROUPS
FOR DEPTH AND DISCOVERY

Companies interested in consumer research frequently use interviews and focus groups to elicit spontaneous and insightful information about attitudes and motivations. These methods are particularly helpful to schools when there is uncertainty about the concerns of various groups or when a misunderstanding of a group's sentiments has led to failed initiatives.

A primary use of interviews and focus groups is as a preliminary research method to discover what issues are important to specific groups, to identify any underlying or unknown concerns, and to reveal opinions and attitudes that can be used to develop more detailed queries.

One-on-one interviews usually involve persons who represent a larger group of people, such as executives of companies or leaders of organizations. Make it clear whether you are seeking the person's personal opinions or those of the group with which she is affiliated.

The typical interview lasts from 45 minutes to one hour. At the time the request for the interview is made, state the purpose of the interview and the topics to be discussed. It is helpful to the person to tell her why she was selected for the interview. For example, "As a key member of the group opposing the latest bond initiative, we believe you can provide greater insight into why the initiative is opposed." Interviews generally are conducted at the interviewee's location. Unless the person objects, tape the interview. It is difficult to interact with the interviewee, ask follow-up questions, and take notes at the same time. Be punctual, come prepared, and do not take more time than you have asked for unless the person indicates that she has more to say. This is not the time for debate. You are there to gather information not try to influence opinion.

Focus groups generally comprise 8–15 people who represent a specific group, such as parents, retired people, students, or a diverse group that represents the demographics of the community. If the purpose is to gather information from external groups, do not include employees of the school or school board members. This can inhibit a free exchange of information. A typical focus group session lasts 1½ to 2 hours.

Unlike interviews and surveys, the group is asked to discuss one or more general topics rather than answer specific questions. The idea is to generate spontaneous dialogue.

The moderator explains the meeting's purpose and objectives. It is important that the participants understand what the school plans to do with the information gathered. The moderator then offers topics for discussion and allows the group to express themselves on each topic. For example, "There has been much in the media lately about the new higher state standards and concerns over testing. We would like to learn what you know about the new standards and your views on how those standards are tested in our schools." To stimulate discussion, the moderator may also show pictures or a film clip or read a brief excerpt from an article.

The moderator participates in the discussion only to keep the conversation going, refocus the discussion if it drifts from the topic, and encourage shy participants to participate. The moderator is not there to debate any subject or correct any misperceptions. The purpose is to gather information. The session is recorded either on audio or video tape. If participants want anonymity, audio tape the session and use first names only.

Research firms, especially those conducting product research, usually pay focus group participants; however, it is likely that the school can find residents who are willing to volunteer their time. I recommend providing refreshments. The sharing of food and drink creates a relaxed atmosphere that can encourage the sharing of opinions and attitudes.

The location of the facility should be convenient and easy to find. Be sure to provide maps to participants who are not familiar with the area. The room should be pleasant and the chairs comfortable. Sitting around a large table or in a circle creates an inclusive feeling and promotes exchanges among the participants. Be sure to send thank you letters to all participants.

Interviews and focus groups offer the following advantages:

- Quality and quantity of information. The greatest advantage of interviews and focus groups is the depth of information they generate. Because participants are not restricted to specific responses to predetermined questions, the amount of information generated can be significant. The probative nature of interviews and focus groups can reveal concerns, feelings, and beliefs previously unknown to the district or school. Not only can you learn how someone feels or what someone thinks, but also why. The school or district can use the information obtained to construct questionnaires that are then disseminated to a larger group.
- Flexibility. The unstructured nature of interviews and focus groups allows the discussion to go in many directions. If a topic seems to be an emotional one that is generating a lot of discussion, the moderator can pursue that avenue. If the discussion stalls, the moderator can take it in another direction or introduce a new topic.
- Rapid results. The gathered data is available for analysis as soon as the audio tapes are transcribed. The gathering and analysis of data can occur within a week.

The disadvantages of interviews and focus groups are:

- Small sample. The major disadvantage, and it is significant, is that the sample or number and type of respondents from interviews and focus groups is very small. It is not likely that the beliefs and opinions of the participants in a few interviews and focus groups will reflect those of the general population.
- Expensive. Effective interviews and focus groups depend on the quality of the questions, the effectiveness of the interviewer or group moderator, and the accuracy of the data analysis. Unless someone in the school has experience in arranging and conducting interviews and focus groups and evaluating the gathered data, it is best to use trained, experienced

interviewers and moderators from a professional research firm. In that case, the per-person costs of interviews and focus groups may exceed those of surveys. If you are using the same research firm to conduct the school's or district's surveys, negotiate to have at least one focus group included at little or no cost.

USE SURVEYS TO REACH LARGER GROUPS

A survey is a systematic method of gathering data about specific topics from a selected group of people. The term *survey* may refer to both the process and the instrument or questionnaire used.

The information gathered from surveys makes significant contributions toward organizational improvement in a number of ways. For example:

- Information: Surveys are one of the most effective and efficient ways to gather specific information on a wide range of topics from both internal and external audiences. Surveys are used to determine satisfaction with the organization, target areas that need improvement, evaluate programs and procedures, and reveal perceptions about the school. A well-designed survey can provide precisely the information the school needs to know for planning, decision-making, and improving relationships with internal and external groups.
- Communication: Surveys promote communication that might not otherwise occur by providing students, employees, parents, and the community an easy and anonymous way to communicate opinions, perceptions, and feelings about a variety of topics. Surveys are also a means to establish communication with people that generally are not in contact with the school. Community-wide surveys are especially useful in gathering information from key groups outside the organization and for establishing communication links between internal groups such as teachers and school administrators.
- Inclusion: Asking people's opinions expresses the value that the school places on its relationship with the community. People like to feel that what they think matters and that others are willing to listen. One of the reasons taxpayers without children in schools are often critical of public education is they feel no connection to it. Surveys are a means to express the school's or school district's willingness to make a connection and confirm the notion that input from internal and external audiences is important to the organization.
- Indicators: Surveys can serve as an early alert system for potential problems or for areas of opportunity. The school can detect shifts in public opinion, areas of growing concern, as well as how internal groups view changes within the organization before they have negative effects. External influences of which the school has no knowledge or control may affect

opinions, perceptions, and relationships over time. Surveys conducted on a regular basis allow the school to track these changes. This kind of information is particularly helpful in improving the school's ability to be proactive rather than reactive.

• Perceptions: Individuals act on perceptions regardless of the reality of circumstances. Surveys offer insight into how various audiences perceive situations vis-à-vis how they really are and how correctly the school is interpreting those perceptions. This is especially true of groups with whom the school has limited contact. Surveys allow misperceptions to be uncovered and corrected before they become entrenched beliefs.

Surveys generally are conducted in three ways: written questionnaires, telephone surveys, and online surveys. Each type is discussed in the following paragraphs.

WRITTEN SURVEYS

Written surveys are one of the most common types of data gathering. The process involves distributing paper questionnaires to the target audiences and then collecting them.

Written surveys have several advantages that make them appealing.

• Low Cost: The cost of producing written questionnaires is pennies per copy, especially if the school reproduces them on its own equipment. The cost of reproducing and distributing questionnaires allows the school to reach a large number of people.

   If the school chooses to produce its own questionnaires, the quality of the copies must be high. Distributing poor quality questionnaires sends a negative message about the importance the school places on the survey process. It is better to have questionnaires printed externally if the school's photocopy equipment cannot produce high-quality copies.

   Written surveys may be sent to and collected from recipients by mail. If respondents must return questionnaires by mail, postage should be included on the questionnaires to achieve a better return rate. To reduce distribution costs, students, parents, and volunteers can deliver and pick up questionnaires from community residents. Questionnaires for parents may be distributed and returned through student take-home packets.

• Ease of completion: Respondents can complete a well-designed questionnaire quickly within their own time schedules; consequently, they are more likely to participate. Because respondents can complete the questionnaire privately when it is convenient, written questionnaires are not perceived to be as intrusive as personal or telephone interviews.

- Greater candor: People may not answer questions about their income, education level, age, or controversial issues truthfully when speaking to an interviewer over the telephone or in person. It is not uncommon for interviewees to say what they think the interviewer wants to hear or to answer in a way that puts themselves in a good light. Respondents are more likely to answer such questions truthfully in an anonymous written questionnaire.
- Ease of tabulation and analysis: Computer software can facilitate data entry, tabulation, and data analysis of written questionnaires. If the process is simple and accurate, the school or district is more likely to conduct research on a regular basis.

Written surveys are not without disadvantages. The most significant are the following:

- Low response rate. Written questionnaires produce the lowest response rate of the commonly used survey methods. This is especially true if questionnaires are distributed and returned via the mail. Even when recipients intend to complete and return the questionnaire, they do not always follow through. It is possible to boost the return rate by delivering and picking up the questionnaires. Use the neighborhood paper or school newsletter to notify survey recipients about the survey and remind them about pickup times.
- Inability to interact with respondent. Telephone interviewers know that some of the best information they receive is when respondents extend their answers beyond what the question asks. This kind of elaboration is rare in written surveys where few people will volunteer more information than is requested. Allowing opportunity for comments in the written questionnaire can lessen this disadvantage, but cannot compensate for the advantage of personal interaction.

  Written questionnaires do not allow the respondent to ask for clarification if the wording is ambiguous or unclear. Any misunderstanding of the questions will result in inaccurate information.
- Inadequate sample. The goal of a public survey is to gather information from a wide range of residents. Generally, people who are motivated to complete and return questionnaires are those who have an interest in the topic or an association with the organization collecting information. The responses to a written questionnaire may not represent the opinions of the total population.

TELEPHONE SURVEYS

Telephone surveys offer some advantages over written surveys.

- Greater sampling. A telephone survey can reach a greater sampling of people, especially if a random dialing system with callback capability is used. Individuals who will not take the time to read and fill out and return a 15–20 minute written questionnaire are frequently willing to participate in a 15–20 minute telephone survey.
- Quick completion time. With good organization and sufficient staff, it is possible to complete a telephone survey in a week. A written survey could take one month or more to distribute and collect.
- Produce more information. It is easier to talk than to write; therefore, people generally provide more information when they give their responses verbally. People who agree to give the interviewer a specified amount of time will often talk much longer and more openly than expected. The personal interaction allows a skilled interviewer to probe for more information. A telephone survey also allows the respondent to ask for clarification of a question, whereas on a written survey the respondent may skip the question or worse give an answer without understanding what is being asked.

Telephone surveys also have disadvantages.

- Cost may be higher than written questionnaires. This is particularly true if an external firm conducts the survey. However, the higher cost may be warranted if you are conducting a major community survey. Because professional research firms have personnel experienced in conducting surveys, multiple phone lines with random dialing capabilities, and tabulation equipment, they generally produce better results than schools and districts that do not have the requisite personnel or equipment. For some participants an external firm offers the notion of impartiality and credibility. Participants may be more willing to provide frank answers to an interviewer not associated with the school or district, and they may have more confidence in the results.
- Respondents have little time to think about their answers. The quickness of completion that makes telephone surveys attractive also has a downside. Prior to the survey, participants may not have spent much time thinking about an issue yet they must provide an immediate response. If the survey deals with complex issues, the result may be a significant number of "don't know" or "no opinion" responses because respondents have neither an opportunity nor enough information to form an opinion.
- Answering machines and cell phones. People often use answering machines to take their calls even when they are available to answer the phone. If the call is not answered, the opportunity to participate is lost. Alerting people through the local media or notices in school communications prior to the survey can improve participation. If possible, give specific days and times when the survey will be conducted. For example, "The community telephone survey

will be conducted during the week of Feb. 2–6 from 7 p.m. to 9 p.m." The increased reliance of cell phones as the sole phone may affect your ability to obtain a wide sample of people unless you have access to the cell phone numbers. Generally, people who have land lines are older or live in areas where cell reception in spotty. Younger people tend to rely solely on cell phones.

ONLINE SURVEYS

As more households gain access to the Internet, electronic surveying has become an attractive option for gathering information. Computer-driven surveys take two forms: e-mail questionnaires sent directly to the target audience and Internet/intranet surveys posted on a webpage. Use e-mail messages to direct the target audience to a webpage that contains the survey. As with other methods, there are advantages and disadvantages.

Online surveys offer the following advantages:
- Cost. Electronic surveys eliminate the cost and effort of producing, distributing, and collecting paper surveys and the personnel and equipment necessary for telephone surveys and substantially decrease the cost of data entry and tabulation costs. The costs are limited to labor attached to questionnaire design and construction. However, in the case of e-mail surveys, unless you possess the e-mail addresses of your audience, you may have to purchase them.
- Speed. Hundreds, even thousands, of surveys can be sent and returned in a day or two via e-mail. Web-based surveys require the respondent to visit the site, but as with e-mail surveys, hundreds even thousands can be gathered in a day or two and the data are instantly input and tabulated.
- Skips are automated. Skips occur when a respondent is requested to skip specific questions based on a previous answer. For example, a question that states, *If you have answered Question 5 as "No," please skip the next three questions.* Webpage surveys (not e-mail surveys) can automatically guide the respondent through the questionnaire to prevent errors.
- Increased response rates. The ease of completing and submitting a computer-based questionnaire, plus their newness, increases the response rate.

Disadvantages include
- Limited access. The use of computer-driven surveys requires that the target audience have e-mail and/or access to the Internet. Those channels may not be available to certain populations. If the respondents are limited to people who have Internet access, the results cannot be generalized to the whole

community. This is becoming less of an issue, but in some areas of the world it may still be a drawback.
• Skewed results. If your questionnaire is on a web page, you do not know who is responding or how many times. People from anywhere in the world can complete the questionnaire multiple times. However, it is possible to require a sign-in process to participate and software is available that prevents people from responding multiple times.

The survey method the school chooses will depend on budget, time constraints, capabilities, and the scope of the data the school wants to collect. No matter what the method of data gathering is, asking the right questions in the right way is critical to collecting useful data. Not only will a set of well-written questions produce high-quality data, but they can also serve as a model for future questions. The following pages contain ways to help the school write its own survey questions or critique those written by an external organization.

ASK THE RIGHT QUESTIONS IN THE RIGHT WAY

A common disappointment with survey results is the realization that the questions did not solicit the needed information. Asking the right questions in the right way is critical whether the survey is written, electronic, or person-to-person. Know exactly what kind of information you want to gather, then form questions that will solicit that information. It sounds simple, but not asking the right questions is one of the most common mistakes in surveys. The result is useless information.

In a written or electronic survey, the respondent cannot ask for help if he does not understand the questions. Therefore it is essential that these surveys contain clearly constructed questions. The chance is far greater that respondents will not complete questionnaires if they find the questions difficult to answer. Below are guidelines to help you word questions properly.

Know what you need to know. Time spent determining exactly what you need to know is time well spent. Knowing whether someone does or does not do something is helpful, even more helpful is knowing why.

If you want to know whether the community finds the school websites useful for finding the information they want, a question such as,

Do you use the school websites for information you need about the school?
Yes   No

will not provide sufficient information to make an informed assessment of the website's effectiveness. A "Yes" response does not necessarily mean that the website is helpful, appealing, or popular. Use does not always imply satisfaction. People may go to the site as a last resort because information they receive through other means is insufficient, not timely, or not helpful. A "No" response is not necessarily a criticism of the site. People may not have Internet access, know what kind of information the site provides, or even know about the site. Getting the right information may require a series of specific questions such as the following:

Do you know that the school has its own website?
Yes   No

If you have used the website, please answer the following questions.
I use the school website to get information I want.

Always   Frequently   Sometimes   Never

I find the information I want.

Always   Frequently   Sometimes   Never

The information I want is easy to find.

Always   Frequently   Sometimes   Never

Eliminate ambiguity. Do not force people to guess what you are asking. Upon first reading, a respondent may understand the following question:

I attend my child's school events.
Yes   No

as referring to *any* or *some* events. On second thought, the respondent wonders if a "yes" answer requires attendance at *all* events. A better approach would be to give the respondent a choice of responses such as:

I attend my child's school events.

Always   Frequently   Sometimes   Never

Ensure that everyone understands the same question in the same way every time. Questionnaire reliability requires that each question be so clearly worded that all respondents will interpret it in the same way every time. Specificity is the key.

Words that have different meanings to different people produce questions that are subject to multiple interpretations. In the question, *Do you communicate often with your child's teacher?* the respondent might interpret the word *often* as anywhere from weekly to once every couple of months. A better question is,

How often do you communicate with your child's teacher during the school year?

More than once a month	Several times a year	Once or twice a year	Not at all

Ask questions people can answer. This may sound like an obvious statement, but often survey questions are written with an assumption that the respondents have certain knowledge, awareness, or understanding that they may not have. A parent may not be able to answer the question, *Has your child experienced bullying at school?* Unless a child chooses to confide in his parents, they may not know whether he has been bullied at school. A possible approach might be to describe signs of emotional distress caused by bullying and ask the parent if the child exhibits any of these signs.

Respondents cannot answer if they do not understand the language that is used. Like many professional groups, educators tend to use jargon, technical terms, or acronyms that are unfamiliar to the community. If you must use such language, clearly explain what it means.

A respondent cannot answer two issues in the same question. It is impossible to give an accurate answer to the question, *Do you find the school staff members courteous and knowledgeable?* if the respondent finds the staff members to have one attribute, but not the other. A better approach is to provide a question that offers specific answers.

In your experiences with school office staff, do you generally find them to be (please check all that apply)

Courteous	Knowledgeable	Helpful	Friendly

Avoid using absolute words such as *everyone, everything, always,* and *never.* It is difficult to answer a question such as, *Do you believe that the state should do everything it can to provide needed technology to our schoolchildren?* A "Yes" response to the phrase "everything it can" suggests the respondent is agreeable to anything the state chooses to do, including raising taxes or cutting other programs. A "No" response suggests the respondent does not believe it is important for the state to help provide technology to schoolchildren.

A question that is too broad, such as *Rate the overall quality of your child's teachers,* is impossible to answer if the respondent considers some teachers as excellent and others as poor. A better question is,

The number of my child's teachers I would rate good to excellent is

All   *Most*   *Some*   *None*

"Yes" or "No" answers may not offer the full range of choices a respondent needs to answer a question precisely. Instead of a yes or no response to the question,

Are you satisfied with the food served in the school cafeteria?

ask the question,

How satisfied are you with the food served in the cafeteria?

Very satisfied   *Somewhat satisfied*   *Not satisfied*

People who take the time to answer a questionnaire want to answer the questions accurately. Questions that are difficult to answer or confusing will produce a negative reaction that may result in noncompletion of the survey.

Avoid leading questions. Do not construct questions with language that leads the respondent to a predetermined answer. Your data will be manipulated and worthless. Special-interest groups that want to use their "results" to prove a point use this type of questioning. Their interest is not in finding accurate data, but rather answers that will support a predetermined point of view. Questions such as *Do you believe that the person who educates your children should be paid less than the person who collects your garbage?* or *Do you think tax dollars should be used to teach easily influenced children about all types of sexual behavior?* leave little doubt as to the "correct" answer.

Even subtle phrasing can create leading and confusing questions. Consider the following two questions:

Do you agree with the city council's decision to oppose limiting construction of new early learning centers?
Do you agree with the city council's decision to support construction of new early learning centers?

Although the questions ask the same thing, they are likely to produce different reactions. It can be difficult to write a neutral question, especially if the issue is a controversial one. It is helpful to have people of differing viewpoints pretest problematic questions.

Provide range questions for demographic information. When giving personal information such as income, age, education levels, people generally feel more comfortable with range questions. For a question regarding income, for example, offer a range such as *Under $20,000, $20,000–$34,999, $35,000–$44,999,* etc. Choose ranges that reflect the income range of the community. Asking questions with specific ranges can avoid ambiguous answers. If you ask, *How long have you lived in the district?* some people may answer, "A long time." Instead, ask *How many years have you lived in the district?* or give ranges such as *Under five years—six to ten years, eleven to fifteen year,* etc. To avoid confusion, be certain that your ranges do not overlap. If the choices for age are 18–25, 25–35, 35–45, etc. the respondent will fall into two categories.

Also consider that some groups may view providing personal information, even anonymously, as invasive or offensive. Individuals may have come from countries where gathering information was politically motivated and intimidating.

Give respondents an opportunity to express themselves. Close-ended questions provide a selection of answers from which the respondent can choose. Open-ended questions allow respondents to come up with their own answers. Because open-ended questions do not limit responses to preset answers, respondents have the opportunity to express themselves in their own words. Open-ended questions can provide some of your most valuable information.

Questions should be easy to understand and answer. Asking people to, "List the three things you like best about our school" or "List the three things you like least about our school" is preferable to asking them to write a short essay on their likes and dislikes concerning the school. In addition, short answers or lists are easier to understand, categorize, and analyze.

Take care not to include too many open-ended questions; two or three should be sufficient. Too many open-ended questions may discourage the respondent and complicate processing results.

Accommodate language differences: If your community has a significant number of non-English speaking residents, questionnaires should be translated to ensure inclusivity. The translation must be precise. There are dozens of funny and not-so-funny examples of what inexact translations actually communicated. With written questionnaires, the respondent does not have the opportunity to ask the meaning of a poorly translated question or phrase. In addition, a poor translation shows a lack of respect for the group's participation.

CREATING GOOD INSTRUMENTS

The quality of the instrument used in a survey has a significant influence on its success in providing meaningful data.

KISS—Keep It Short and Simple. A 15-page questionnaire will discourage participation. Low participation will result in data that are of little value. It is better to use a few shorter surveys spread out over time than one huge survey.

Keep the length of the questionnaire to no more than four double-sided pages, shorter if it addresses a single issue such as school safety or volunteer satisfaction. Respondents are more likely to complete a questionnaire that appears to take no more than 10–15 minutes.

Look at each question and ask yourself why you need this information and what you will do with it. If you cannot find sufficient reason to keep it, take it out.

Make the questionnaire appealing. The overall look of the questionnaire can influence the response rate. Create a cover sheet that contains the school logo or an attractive, professional looking graphic design along with the school name, survey date (Spring 2015), and survey title. Use a heavier weight of paper in a pale color such as gray or cream for the cover page and add some color to the text or artwork. You want the respondent to take your survey seriously; so, avoid comic or cute clip art.

The first time the respondent looks at the questionnaire, he sees it as a whole. Use enough white space in the margins and keep the questions well spaced to prevent an overcrowded, mind-numbing look.

The type should be 11 or 12 point in an easy-to-read font. Use a high-quality paper and have the questionnaire photocopied at a professional copy center if the school's copy equipment does not product crisp, clear copies. Fuzzy, faded type on poor quality paper creates a poor impression of the school and the survey.

Begin the questionnaire with clear instructions on how to complete it. Use short sentences and basic words. If the instructions are too complicated, the respondent may become discouraged even before he gets started. The first few questions should be simple to answer and noncontroversial.

Once the respondent is engaged in completing the questionnaire, it is likely that he will finish it even if the questions become more complex. However, avoid putting the most important questions at the end of the questionnaire in the event that the respondent fails to finish.

Group questions together that have the same response options (yes/no, multiple choice, ranking, fill-in-the-blank). Changing the response format frequently is tiring to the respondent.

Group items into logically coherent sections. Jumping from one issue to another can make the questionnaire seem confusing and unfocused. Keeping all questions related to a specific topic or issue together helps the respondent understand the rationale behind the questions.

Number the questions and number the pages (include the total number of pages, e.g., page 2 of 4) in case the questionnaire pages become detached. Printing on both sides will hold down costs and give the respondent fewer pages to keep track of.

Include an introduction letter. To introduce the questionnaire, insert a cover letter that states the purpose of the survey, how the school intends to use the data, the importance of participation, and appreciation of the respondent's participation. For example, a letter accompanying a communication survey might read as follows:

Dear Parent or Guardian,
We at Lincoln Middle School know it is important to communicate with the parents and guardians of our students. It is also important that you are able to communicate with us. You can help us determine how well we are communicating and how we can improve by answering the questions on the enclosed **Communication Survey.**

Your answers will be used to help us determine the best way to create and maintain good two-way communication with you. It is important that you answer all questions including the demographic information. The questionnaires are anonymous to ensure the confidentiality of your responses.

Please return the questionnaire in the enclosed envelope before October 25, 2015. We will report the results of the survey on the school Websites and in our school newsletter.

The administration and staff at Lincoln Middle School appreciate the time you give to complete this questionnaire and we thank you for your participation. If you have any questions, please contact the survey coordinator, Cindy Butler, at 713.555.5535 or at her school E-mail address cbutler@lincolnms. edu.

Sincerely,
Amelia Flores, Principal

If the survey is conducted electronically, state the purpose of the survey, how the school intends to use the data, the importance of participation, and appreciation of the respondent's participation at the beginning of the survey. If the survey is conducted by telephone, have the same elements in a statement that the interviewer reads to the participant.

Guarantee confidentially. Even when the survey does not involve controversial or emotional issues, people should feel confident that the information and opinions they provide cannot be linked to them. This is particularly important if school personnel conduct the survey or if school employees are surveyed. Understandably, school employees, students, even parents may be reluctant to express honest opinions if they feel that administrators have access to their individual responses. State, in the cover letter or in the questionnaire, that participation is anonymous.

Always pretest questionnaires. The best way to ensure that the questions meet the necessary requirements is to have questions pretested by individuals who are similar to the ones you want to survey. Gather a small group and go through each question to ensure that the questions are worded correctly, the response choices are appropriate, and the instructions are clear. If the respondents speak languages other than English, ensure that the translations are of the highest quality and that the questions are culturally acceptable.

PRESURVEY COMMUNICATION

Alerting the target audience that the school or school district will conduct a survey can boost participation significantly. If the survey audience is limited to the school's community, a presurvey postcard or flyer explaining the purpose of the survey and the importance of participation should be mailed a week to 10 days before the survey is conducted. To encourage people to return written questionnaires, send out follow-up postcards two weeks after the initial survey distribution. A PDF copy of the questionnaire posted on the school or district websites allows respondents who have lost or misplaced the questionnaire to print copies. Use social media to promote the survey and send reminders.

An article or news spot in local or social media channels before a community survey can stress the importance of involvement and increase the participation rate. Provide information on the purpose of the survey and how and when it will be conducted. After a major community survey, issue a press release reviewing the results and explain how the district or school intends to respond to the results.

TIMING MAY NOT BE EVERYTHING, BUT IT IS IMPORTANT

When and how often to conduct surveys depends largely on the type of survey. An annual survey to determine parents' or students' satisfaction will be more fruitful when conducted at the end of the school year. The school is likely to have greater participation and receive answers that are more reflective if it conducts teacher surveys during holiday and vacation periods when teachers have more time.

Consider how recent events might skew data. The best time to conduct a survey regarding new policies and procedures is not immediately after implementation. Allow people time to adjust to the changes and experience the benefits. A survey a few months after the changes will give a better view of how the changes are being accepted.

It is not necessary to conduct research before each marketing decision. A few well-constructed surveys should provide the school with the information it needs to make sound decisions for some time. If the marketing team has completed the school assessment, it should know what areas require more decision-making information.

Conduct shorter surveys related to single issues such as volunteer satisfaction once a year, especially if there is significant turnover. A major district survey of the community every five years should be sufficient unless major issues or changes have occurred. Conducting surveys more frequently will not be worth the money and effort and can cause survey burnout in your target audiences.

IS IT LEGAL?

Before conducting student surveys, check your state's regulations. Some states require parental consent for student questionnaires. Recently, parents filed and won a suit against a Texas school district to stop surveys that they considered intrusive. The parents felt that the surveys invaded not only the privacy of the student but the student's family as well. Students whose parents complained suffered retaliation. No information is so valuable that it justifies forcing students to participate in surveys that create divisiveness in the community. Moreover, the school or district may find itself facing legal action.

In addition to obtaining parental consent, districts can reduce objections by creating a committee of parents and school staff to review potentially sensitive questionnaires and allow parents the option to review questionnaires prior to giving consent.

SURVEY WARNINGS

When conducting research, consider some of the following pitfalls common to information gathering.

Hidden agendas foster cynicism. If motives other than the stated ones exist, they jeopardize the credibility of future research. If a school's stated goal for gathering public opinion is to gather information to help it make informed decisions, but the hidden motive is to use the information to create manipulative messages, the school endangers future initiatives. In the same way that voters have become distrustful of political groups that use information from opinion polls to construct messages to play on voters' emotions, hidden agendas can create a public that is cynical about the school. Clearly state objectives and adhere to them.

A survey that tries to satisfy everyone will satisfy no one. Research becomes unwieldy when it attempts to meet everyone's needs. To provide useful information, a survey should explore a few important issues thoroughly rather than many superficially. It is better to prioritize objectives and conduct multiple research projects over time.

The goal is not to produce predetermined results. Circumstances sometimes make it tempting to use tactics designed to provide the desired research results. I already have addressed how the wording of questions can lead respondents to the desired answer. Another way to sway results is to select a survey sample that is likely to produce the preferred outcome. If a district or school wishes to substantiate the claim that its teachers feel safe in the classroom, a survey that limits its sample primarily to elementary school teachers or teachers in schools with no reports of teacher intimidation is likely to support that claim. The survey results, however, are useless and deceptive. A critical analysis of the survey instrument and the methodology will reveal the intent to manipulate results. Research conducted in this manner damages credibility.

Research results should lead to action. If a colleague continually asks for your advice and opinion about how he could improve his performance, but he never makes any change for the better, eventually you would come to view his requests as a waste of your time and his. When school or district administrators ask for opinions and perceptions, the assumption is that they will use the information to facilitate planning, initiate improvements, and make informed decisions. Gathering information does not mean you are letting other people make your decisions, it means you are allowing them to have input into what decisions are made.

If the information gathered is never used, participants will see the effort as a waste of time and resources. They will be less likely to participate in the future. This is particularly true of audiences such as school staff members, parents, and students who are mostly closely affected by school or district decisions.

WHEN TO GET HELP

The school should be able to handle most small surveys related to single issues or specific audiences such as volunteer satisfaction, employee and student satisfaction, or effective communication channels. However, conducting a major research project such as a community-wide survey in a large urban area can seem like an overwhelming task. That is one reason why administrators avoid them. If uncertainty about the school's or district's ability to conduct a survey is an obstacle to gathering needed information, consider getting help from a research company.

Another reason to consider external help is to convey a sense of impartiality and anonymity. Some survey audiences are more likely to participate and to respond frankly if a third party, not affiliated with the school or district, conducts the survey. Employees, for example, may not be forthcoming regarding satisfaction with their supervisors and work environment if district personnel conduct the survey unless they can be guaranteed anonymity. As tempting as it may be, you really do not want respondents to tell you what they think you want to hear.

Larger towns and cities have marketing research firms that can provide consulting services or handle the entire project. You can find companies that specialize in school research on the Internet. In addition to questionnaires for a variety of audiences, these companies provide assistance with focus groups and in-depth interviews, evaluations and needs assessment, and other consultation services.

If the school decides to use an external firm, pick three or four and interview them to evaluate their level of relevant experience, ability to carry out the project, understanding of education issues, and price. A good firm will appreciate the school's limited resources and suggest ways to get the most for the dollars spent.

If the school decides to conduct its own surveys, the Internet is an excellent resource for locating both other schools and districts that have conducted community, student, and parent surveys and companies that specialize in school-based surveys. Questionnaires specific to school issues are available for purchase and can be modified to meet your school's specific requirements.

DATA-DRIVEN MARKETING

Data can be used in two ways to market your school. One way involves the collection, analysis, and dissemination of statistical school-related data. The other way involves the organization of data related to external groups within the district or school environment.

Individuals make decisions based on information. But, people in the community are not all looking for the same kind of information. Parents who are deciding where their child will attend elementary school want information that is different from a student deciding where she will attend high school.

Parents may want data on students' performance on state accountability tests, teacher-student ratios, percentage of teachers with advanced degrees, or special programs. The high school student may want to know about advanced placement or honors classes, extracurricular activities, or the amount of technology in the school. Even among parents, the criteria for school selection may vary. The demographic makeup of the student and teachers, availability of bilingual programs, or incidents of violence may be of concern. Companies considering relocation want specific kinds of information about the local schools or district such as the district's rating, graduation rates, student performance on exit exams, and collaborative programs between businesses and schools. Teachers looking for positions may want to know about class sizes, staff turnover, professional development programs, or the percentage of staff with advanced degrees.

All schools collect and maintain statistical data for their own internal use. In marketing your school, knowing what kinds of information the various external groups want to obtain and being able to provide it readily is critical. Establishing a source of appropriate data will allow the school to respond quickly to requests for information. When the school makes frequently requested data available, in paper form or on the school's website, the message is that the school considers this information valuable to the community.

A second kind of database allows the school to assemble information about the various groups within the school's environment, sort and store the information, and retrieve specific segments quickly. Several database software programs are available that make the process of inputting and retrieving data uncomplicated. The software consolidates the input data in a file and allows for quick retrieval of specific segments as required. A typical process might be as follows:

- Build a list of everyone the school may want to contact at some time.
- Input basic contact information such as names and addresses. For some groups, such as parents, volunteers, and key communicators, include telephone and fax numbers and e-mail addresses.
- Determine the categories you want to establish. Examples of categories are:
  Parents
  Parents of children in your school's feeder pattern
  Parents with children not in your school
  Contacts in the business community
  Volunteers
  PTO members
  Retired people
  Alumni

There are marketing benefits attached to using a database. Being able to retrieve particular segments of the database allows the school to send specific messages to a small group or general information to a larger group or groups. Communication can be personalized. The speed of data retrieval allows for rapid distribution of information in a crisis. It is advantageous to have "crisis communication" indicators attached to names of parents, local agencies, hospitals, key communicators, even the media so their information can be retrieved and disseminated to them quickly.

The ease of data retrieval promotes proactive communication. Consider the following example of how database information could help in the marketing process by targeting specific groups with a specific message.

Riverside High School is holding an open house. The school would like to use this occasion to begin recruiting middle school students for its new *Scientists in the Making* program. The school obtains from its central administration the names and addresses of middle school students who live within a five-mile radius of the school. Students and their parents are invited to Riverside High School's open house to meet with school representatives and receive an introduction to the *Scientists in the Making* program. The school asks students and parents who attend to register. Their names and addresses are put into the school's database. During the year, these students and their families are sent updates on what is happening in the *Scientists in the Making* program and invitations to science-related activities.

Good information is essential to all aspects of school marketing. Marketing research can ensure that the information used is accurate and current. Database marketing then allows the school to use the information in a systematic way to maximize the effectiveness of the school's message.

Chapter 4

Marketing Communication

We cannot *not* communicate. Everything we do or say communicates something, including absolute silence. Even space and time send messages. A spacious office with a bank of windows overlooking a city skyline communicates something about the status of the occupant. How much time we are willing to give to a meeting communicates the importance we place on the subject and the participants. International diplomacy is rife with nonverbal indicators that communicate the significance of events. Who meets with whom, where, and for how long can have global implications.

We cannot *uncommunicate*. Once we have communicated something, we can apologize, rephrase, embellish, or deny, but we cannot undo the communication act. As a result, all communication has consequences attached to it. Situations may exist when no explicit communication is the best course of action until the situation changes. However, an avoidance of communication carries its own message. Just ask someone who has received the "silent treatment."

Communication is at the heart of marketing. It is not overstating the importance of communication to say that if your school is not communicating well, it is not marketing well. Your school may have valuable benefits to offer students, parents, and the community, but if the audience cannot or is not willing to read or listen to the message, those attributes may remain unknown. Communication takes many forms: verbal and nonverbal, written and spoken, images and symbols, interpersonal, group, and mass communication. All forms are important and should be given consideration when constructing communication.

UNDERSTANDING THE COMMUNICATION PROCESS

Communication is both a simple and a complex process. It is simple in that the process includes few steps. Harold Laswell, a social scientist, suggested that the entire process could be summarized by answering the following questions:

Who? Says what? Using what channel? To whom? With what result?

In a communication model, the sender or source constructs a message then sends it via a channel to a receiver who interprets it. The receiver then provides feedback in some form to the sender. The feedback could be an action, a response to the message, or no action or response at all, which also communicates something.

Communication is a never-ending process. Communication received by the sender prior to sending his message influences how he encodes or constructs his message. How the receiver interprets or decodes the message will influence her feedback to the sender and messages she sends to others. The complex nature of communication derives from the variables at each stage that affect the quality of the communication.

If the principal, Mr. Jenkins, received a message from a concerned parent regarding a serious emotional issue with her child, the information contained in the parent's message influences how Mr. Jenkins (sender) constructs a message (message encoded) that he sends via e-mail (channel) to Ms. Chatham, the school counselor (receiver). Ms. Chatham then interprets the message (message decoded) and responds to Mr. Jenkins (feedback). The information received in the message from Mr. Jenkins will influence how Ms. Chatham constructs her message when she communicates with the concerned parent.

Variables at each stage of the communication process can affect the effectiveness of the communication process. For example, if Mr. Jenkins does not construct his message in a way that conveys the seriousness of the situation, Ms. Chatham may not respond in a timely manner, thereby exacerbating the situation.

The sender may be an individual, group, or even an organization that has a message to communicate. Sender variables are characteristics that influence what symbols (words, gestures, signs) the sender uses to encode the message. Sender variables include age, gender, education level, nationality, profession, race, even an emotional state in the case of individuals and structural characteristics and specific agendas in the case of groups or organizations. A school administrator would likely use different language than a middle-school student to communicate the same idea.

Communication will be more effective when the sender constructs or encodes the message with symbols that are meaningful and persuasive to the receiver. If the district is communicating with the community to persuade them of the merits of a bond issue, how the message sent to senior taxpayers is encoded might differ from the one sent to parents with children in the school. In bond elections, encoding may have legal restrictions. It is, however, sometimes difficult for the sender not to be overly influenced by his own characteristics and specific circumstances as he constructs a message. When constructing a message, it is essential, to the greatest extent possible, to consider how the receiver will interpret it. For this reason, it is important to know as much as possible about your audiences.

The channel is the method used to deliver the message. Some channels are more effective in delivering a particular kind of message than others. Information of interest to the general public is delivered best via channels (television, radio, newspapers) where people generally look for news. In addition, traditional news sources provide a level of credibility. Communication to specific groups can be delivered effectively using face-to-face presentations or teleconferencing. Personal messages are generally best communicated one-to-one, although the novelty of proposing marriage via a billboard has sometimes resulted in the desired response.

When choosing a channel, consider the variables that may determine how effective it will be. A public relations campaign I worked on required that we convey a message concerning a special fund-raising event to the parents of schoolchildren. Despite our reservations, the school insisted that information concerning the event be sent home with the children. Their main consideration regarding the delivery channel was cost; ours was reliability. The event was only partially successful, because only about 30 percent of the parents received the message. Students forgot to give their parents the information or lost it. By the time the school realized the inefficiency of the delivery system, it was too late to take corrective action. The variable, in this case, was the degree of the channel (student) reliability.

To ensure channel reliability it is best to use multiple channels. For example, if the school wants to convey information concerning a critical health issue, the situation may require that, in addition to messages sent home with children, channels include e-mails or automated telephone calls to parents, news stories in the media, announcements made through health or local religious organizations, social media, and bulletins on the school website.

When selecting channels for school communications evaluate their effectiveness by asking these questions: Is the channel available to the intended receiver? Is the channel one that the intended receiver is likely to use? Is the channel one considered credible by the receiver? Is the channel reliable? In the example above, using only e-mail or social media to convey critical health information is not effective if there are parents who don't have access to it.

If you choose personal interaction, such as a presentation to a group or a one-on-one conversation, as your channel, you are communicating nonverbally as well as verbally. Nonverbal communication, such as facial expressions, body movements and gestures, tone of voice, emphasis on certain words, and pauses, sends a message that parallels the verbal one. If the nonverbal communication is inconsistent with the verbal, your message will be mixed and ineffective. An administrator who professes interest in a parent's concerns, but continues to take telephone calls and fiddle with paperwork during the meeting is sending a mixed message that communicates insincerity and lack of interest.

The next step in the communication process is decoding by the receiver. An important truism to remember in creating effective communication is that all communication is receiver based. The message you send is not necessarily the message that is received. Message interpretation is subject to the receiver's mental filters. These mental filters are influenced by the same factors that may influence the sender, such as language, culture, level of education, emotional state, age, gender, or economic status. To communicate effectively, it is necessary to have an awareness of filters that might influence the receiver's interpretation of the message. Is your message one that your audience will understand, accept, and find persuasive?

Some filters, such as an emotion, may be temporary. Other filters, such as language or education level, may be lasting or change slowly over time.

Feedback is always sent to the sender by the receiver. Even if the receiver says nothing and walks away from the sender, feedback has occurred. Sometime, a sender can be so focused on his own message that he ignores feedback. However, feedback provides important clues regarding the interest, understanding, and receptivity of the sender's message. If a sender is attentive to the feedback, he can determine if the intended message was conveyed, and if not, take corrective action.

If attendance at the school open house is low among a certain segment of the parents, it could be that the parents did not understand the message, did not recognize the importance of it, or did not know if they would be welcome or comfortable at the event. If low attendance is reoccurring, this is a signal that your message is not being received as you intended.

CHOOSE YOUR WORDS CAREFULLY

Words are powerful. Words have instigated some of humans' most noble and ignoble deeds. Words can change, shape, even create reality. Remember the children's defiant retort, "Sticks and stones can break my bones, but words can never hurt me." Even as children, we knew it was not true. Words can hurt. Words have denigrated entire groups of people, but they also have inspired others to rise above oppression.

Choose your words carefully. Words the school uses in its messages set a tone that affects how audiences view it. Most schools I visit have a sign at the entrance that requests that visitors go to the school office to sign in and receive a visitor badge. In some instances, the language in these signs is so inhospitable that I feel like an intruder. The wording of the sign creates a negative emotional response that influences my perception of how welcome visitors are even before I enter the school. If such language is pervasive, it can dissuade a hesitant parent from visiting the school.

Consider how school communications to parents, staff members, and students are worded. Do requests or directions have a positive or negative tone? *Locker doors should be kept closed and locked* is preferable to *Do not leave lockers open or unlocked.* A message that tells parents, *We can accept only checks or money orders for activities fees* is preferable to *We will not accept cash or credit cards for activities fees.*

It may seem like a small thing; but, the words the school chooses create an effect that influences how the receiver reacts to current and future messages. How the receiver reacts influences how the receiver responds. It is worth the effort to assess how wording affects the tone of school communications.

IT'S ALL ABOUT THE RECEIVER

Effective communication is receiver focused. A message may describe all the school's attributes and benefits, but the message will not be effective if it does not communicate the attributes and benefits in a way that the audience finds logical, emotionally appealing, and credible. This is one reason why it is so important to know and understand the various audiences in your community.

Always keep the receiver in mind when creating messages. Too often the sender concentrates on what he wants the audience to know rather than what the audience wants to know. If the communication piece is an invitation to a school event, the sender may consider the time, place, and type of activity to be the most important items to communicate. If the receivers are new immigrants, their concerns may be whether they will be able to communicate with other attendees, if they will feel comfortable, and why attending is important for their children.

Use words, ideas, and images to which your audience can relate. Do not use jargon or technical words. Appeal to the values of your audience. For schools, pictures of children are always appealing, especially if the pictures are of children attending the school. Include not only photographs of students, but also staff members, volunteers, and parents of various national and ethnic groups. If you feel that you do not have sufficient knowledge about a particular group to create effective messages, request assistance from business people, cultural organizations, religious leaders, or agency workers who are familiar with the target audience.

Let us say that your school has a significant number of Spanish-speaking students. Past attendance of their parents at school events has been low. You want a communication piece that will encourage these parents to come to an open house. Certainly, your invitation should be in Spanish as well as in English. Use Spanish that is free of slang and idioms. Slang and idioms used in Mexico may have different meanings to people from Central or South America.

Send the invitation from the students as well as the administration and staff members. If you use photographs in your communication piece, use pictures of school activities that would be of particular interest to the families and include Hispanic students, parents, and teachers.

Stress the family aspect of the open house and the importance of the child's family in his/her school life. The goal is for the parents to feel that if they attend they will feel welcome and be able to communicate their expectations and concerns to people who understand not only their language, but also their values. Most of all parents should feel that their participation will benefit their children.

It is also important that students understand that their parents are welcome. Children may experience anxiety if there is doubt about how their parents will be treated by the staff members and other parents. Use students as one of your channels of communication by sending invitations home with them, positively promote the event in their classes, and encourage them to prepare work to show to their parents.

In some cases, special attention may be needed for groups who have recently suffered great personal loss and displacement from war and political or religious persecution. The school staff members may feel ill-equipped to create messages that will communicate effectively with these groups. Help can come from social clubs, religious organizations, or assistance agencies that have close interaction with the groups. Inclusion in their children's school activities may ease the emotion of being separated from friends, family, and homeland and help them adapt to a new environment.

When developing communication, do not think in terms of large groups of people. Even though you may be communicating with a large group, imagine one person, the kind of person you want to reach, seeing or listening to your communication; then try to put yourself in his or her place. If necessary, get input from someone who matches the "profile" of the audience you are trying to reach. When the message is part of a major initiative, use surveys or focus groups composed of members of your target audience such as students or senior taxpayers to gain an understanding of what the groups think. This information will help you construct messages that will appeal to their interests and information needs.

We often create messages based on how *we* would view or understand them. This is like giving someone a gift because it is something that you want without consideration for the receiver's desires. The key is to construct your message with the recipient in mind.

EFFECTIVE COMMUNICATION IS TWO-WAY

Imagine that you and I are having a conversation; however, I do virtually all the talking. I speak about the subjects that are important to me, interrupt you frequently, and when you speak, my actions and responses indicate that I have little interest in what you are saying. Are we communicating effectively? I may think so; however, I doubt that you would. How would this type of interaction make you feel? Would you be inclined to repeat the experience if you had a choice?

This is how many organizations communicate. The organization believes it is communicating when it sends lots of information about itself to various groups with great regularity. School communications involve sending a steady stream of notices, bulletins, reports, and announcements about the school and its students. That is as it should be. However, if opportunities for incoming communication are limited primarily to parent/teacher conferences or the annual open house, the school is sending a message that it is not interested in hearing from its audiences and, moreover, it is denying itself valuable, even essential, information.

The importance of acquiring comments, reactions, evaluations, inquiries, and data from internal and external audiences warrants an assessment of the school's ability and desire to seek such information and a plan to correct any deficiencies.

Below are some suggested questions for conducting an assessment.

- What channels for incoming communication does the school currently have in place?
- How do most people choose to communicate with the school? Telephone? Website? Visits? Events?
- Are communication channels easy to access?
- Does the school actively solicit or encourage incoming communication? How?
- What is the response time for inquires by telephone? Website? E-mail? In writing?

- Does the school have communication goals and policies? Are staff members aware of the goals and policies?
- What initiatives are there for personal interaction? How frequent are they?
- Does the school know the satisfaction level of people who communicate with the school? How does the school gather this information?

After the evaluation is complete, ask your audiences for their assessment. This can be done through informal channels such as conversations and meetings or through a formal survey. Then compare results. How well do they match? Are there major inconsistencies? A school may view its website as an excellent channel of communication, but external audiences may not know about it, find it difficult to navigate, or not have the ability to access it. The administration may advocate open communication with employees, but provide few secure opportunities for input.

Employees can be one of the most effective channels for collecting information. As members of social, religious, and special-interest groups within the community, employees can be eyes and ears for the school. Employees' spouses who work within the school's community have access to larger, more varied groups of people. The kinds of comments and questions they receive can provide insight about the concerns, opinions, and perceptions the public holds about issues related to the school.

Getting out of your school and into the community offers administrators excellent opportunities to solicit input. Whether you are making a formal presentation before a homeowners association or having a casual conversation at a civic club luncheon, use the occasion to ask for input.

Channels for incoming communication should offer positive experiences for the user. Invite communication only through channels that you feel confident will provide constructive interaction. If people are encouraged to submit questions or comments via an *Inquiry Line* on the school website, but the site is difficult to navigate and messages are not acknowledged, the channel is counterproductive. Not only will people not use it, they will have doubts about the school's sincerity to get their input.

Within this chapter several avenues for creating two-way communication are described. Even with limited resources, a beneficial level of reciprocal communication is achievable.

THE OSTRICH SYNDROME

I once faced stiff opposition to conducting employee and community satisfaction surveys for an organization from its public information officer. There was concern that public confidence had declined and the organization felt a survey was warranted. The public information officer, however, was afraid that any disapproving results would make it into the news and result in negative publicity. Fortunately, the organization understood that sticking one's head in the sand, and hoping problems will just disappear, is neither good marketing nor good policy. The survey was not as negative as the public relations officer anticipated and it yielded some unexpected input that allowed the organization to better serve its stakeholders.

One benefit of two-way communication is that it allows organizations to be proactive rather than reactive. When information flows in through formal and informal channels, the district or school can become aware of situations before they become issues or problems. It is preferable to find out about and address a problem or issue before it is an item presented to the school board or ends up as a negative story in the local paper. Parents, employees, students, and the community can provide insight about community perceptions and issues that the school might not be aware of otherwise. However, these groups will provide that information only if they feel that the school encourages and is honestly interested in gathering information from their constituencies.

Consider the following situation. A middle-school principal, who encourages input from school employees, hears that bullying in the school is becoming more than just the occasional flexing of adolescent egos. She gets with her marketing team to work out a proactive communication strategy to address the potential problem on multiple levels. The school calls upon local law enforcement specialists, school security, and mental health professionals for their expertise. Policies are established regarding bullying in the school and these are communicated to all employees, students, and parents in a variety of mediums. Confidential communication channels are set up for individuals to report incidents of bullying. School employees and parents receive guidelines for detecting the behavior patterns of the perpetrators or the recipients of bullying. Teachers, with the guidance of counselors, are requested to address bullying in their classrooms. Incidents of bullying are investigated and dealt with quickly.

Through a proactive approach, situations with the potential to harm students and the school were diffused. Does this approach guarantee that no incidents will ever occur? No, but the likelihood is diminished.

Many of us have a tendency to ignore unpleasant issues until forced to address them. Consider the lines of stressed-out taxpayers at post offices on April 15th. However, if I file my taxes late, I am the one who suffers the consequences. In a school environment, not acting in advance of problems can adversely affect a multitude of people. Being proactive can lessen the chances of an occurrence becoming a crisis.

MIXED MESSAGES, MIXED RESULTS

Talk is cheap. Actions speak louder than words. If you talk the talk, you should walk the walk. Pick your favorite truism. If the school does not back up its "talk" with action, it could prove detrimental.

A school that says it welcomes visitors, but offers no place for them to park, has staff members that are rude or indifferent, and provides no visitor information is sending conflicting messages. A school that encourages people to volunteer but does not provide meaningful work or offer recognition for their efforts demonstrates insincerity. Inconsistency between message and action results in a loss of credibility.

Once credibility is lost, it is difficult to reestablish. Loss of credibility in one area can spill over onto others. Think about the messages sent internally and externally and honestly ask if the school can and will back them up with action. Following through with action sends a powerful message that your messages have merit.

Message consistency also provides credibility. Audiences feel they can rely on what is being communicated when there is no deviation from the message. The importance of consistency is evident in political campaigns. Staying "on message" is a major goal. Candidates frequently try to catch their opponents making conflicting statements or saying one thing and doing another so they can assail each other's credibility, the implication being that what the candidate is saying now cannot be trusted because last month he said something different. That may or may not be the case, but public perception may be swayed nevertheless.

Mixed messages generally result from a lack of focus. Having clear goals is essential to message consistency. If school safety is an issue in the community and the message is that one of the district's goal is to make safety a priority, then that message should be reinforced throughout the district in multiple ways until it is no longer an issue or concern.

If you have been on the receiving end of mixed messages, you know how confusing, frustrating, and counterproductive they are. When people say one thing and do another or when messages are constantly changing, they come to have little meaning or importance. Staying "on message" is possible for the school or district when goals are clear and consistently articulated. The marketing team should monitor messages and activities to ensure that they are consistent with stated objectives.

THE VALUE OF ONE-ON-ONE COMMUNICATION

One-on-one communication is powerful. Chances are a principal reason you continue to patronize a particular dry cleaners, auto mechanic, bank, financial planner, or florist is that you have come to know and trust them through personal contact and service. Would you take your business elsewhere just because you received a glossy, attractive brochure in the mail? Probably not. Flyers, brochures, and newsletters can be effective communication pieces, but they are not a replacement for personal communication. People form their strongest opinions through one-on-one contact.

When a principal found that some of her students' parents were considering a nearby private school, she did not send them a letter or brochure. The principal invited the parents to come for individual meetings. Through these meetings, the principal found out that the private school was marketing heavily to all the parents.

The private school's marketing concentrated on their special character-education program that appealed to these parents. Personal meetings gave the principal the opportunity to tell the parents about the character-education program that her school had initiated and to show them the curriculum and supporting materials. The parents also appreciated that their children's continued attendance at the school warranted personal meetings with the principal. As a result of the meetings, all of the parents left their children in the school. An additional benefit of the personal meetings was the information gathered from the parents. From parents' comments, the principal realized the school needed to communicate better regarding school initiatives and programs and that research on the school's competition would be beneficial.

Teachers and school staff have many opportunities at school functions, teacher conferences, sporting events, and holiday parties to form positive impressions of the school through one-on-one communication. If it becomes apparent that interaction between school personnel and parents is lacking, it is to the school's benefit to provide training in customer service, public relations, and effective communication to teachers and staff members and encourage them to become goodwill ambassadors for the school.

CLEARING THE HURDLES TO EFFECTIVE COMMUNICATION

All forms of communication face obstacles in attracting and holding someone's attention. Competition from other sources is the most obvious obstacle. Individuals are bombarded daily with messages from every medium, direct mail, radio, television, billboards, magazines, and the Internet. The school's message is like one in a group of children all jumping up and down, waving their hands shouting "Me! Me! Pick me!"

Not only must the school compete with the barrage of other messages, but it must also compete with the other activities in the audience's lives. The activity-filled lives people lead leave little time to give any message much attention. Think of yourself going through the pieces of mail you receive every day. How much time are you willing to give to each piece before you discard it or keep it to read? It is likely that initially each piece will receive no more than a few seconds of your time. Unless you are particularly interested in the subject matter, you are not likely to give much time to processing the message. It is important to convey the school's message quickly and in a way that will attract and hold the receiver's interest.

To secure the receiver's attention, the message must stand out. Again, think about the pieces of mail that come to you each day or the multitude of commercials on television. Why do you notice one of these above the many? People are attracted to a message for any of several reasons. The message is relevant to something that is of interest to them, it creates a strong emotional feeling, it is striking or unconventional, it is humorous, or it is simply too clever to be ignored. The school's communication must be one that will stand out and hold the receiver's attention long enough to convey the message.

When a large urban district was facing a teacher shortage, the critical nature of the situation required more than the usual recruitment activities. A local advertising agency agreed to conduct a recruitment campaign at a reduced fee for the district. The results exceeded expectations.

Although many factors contributed to the campaign's success, including a generous sign-on bonus, an effective communication piece was a critical instrument in developing an awareness of the recruitment effort. Rather than rely just on traditional ads in the usual recruitment venues such as classified ads and online employment sites, the agency chose eye-catching billboards along major freeways and signage on mass transit vehicles where competition was less likely. By using billboards and bus signage, the agency put the message in front of people on their way to and from work who might be considering new career opportunities.

The billboard and signs comprised a black background with white and yellow text. Hard to miss. One third of the sign displayed a black and white photograph of an engaging child looking out at the viewer. On the remaining two-thirds in white text were the words, "Will **You** Be My **Teacher**?" The words "You" and "Teacher" were emphasized with larger, yellow text. The only other text on the sign provided the name of the district and a telephone number.

The photographic image of the child initially attracted attention. The simple layout and text of the advertisements allowed the reader to scan the message and understand the requested action quickly, a requirement for an appeal to people, in this case literally, on the move. Asymmetrical design attracted the eye to the main message. The eye then moved from the message to the sender of the message (district name) and the request for action (telephone number) in a matter of seconds.

The ads were visually and emotionally appealing in an unconventional way. The message was not the typical employment ad from a school district requesting the audience to consider teaching, but rather an array of eye-catching children of different races and ages asking simply and directly, "Will **you** be my **teacher**?" The face of an engaging child with a clear and touching request was sure to stand out from the usual employment ads. Atypical colors of black and yellow created a dramatic visual effect that distinguished the ads from their surroundings even in the clutter of competing signage.

In summary, the message was effective because it stood out from the competition in both form and placement, it took only seconds to read, understand, and solicit a response, and the design was dramatic, touching, and personal. It cleared the three hurdles of competition, time, and sameness.

LOGOS—PATHOS—ETHOS

Rhetoric, the art of effective expression and the use of persuasive language, goes back centuries. In *Rhetoric*, his first major work on the subject written in the 4th century B.C.E., Aristotle noted three components of persuasive communication, logos (logic), pathos (emotion), and ethos (credibility). Like much of what we inherited from the ancient Greeks, these ideas are still sound today. To be persuasive, a message, whether written or spoken, should be substantively sound, emotionally appealing, and from a source the audience considers credible.

The importance of these elements in creating persuasive communication requires that we spend some time examining each of them.

Logic. Logic requires that persuasive communication be reasonable, make the connection between ideas, define problems and offer solutions, show cause and effect, and provide information to validate the argument. In short, logic demands that the message make sense to the sender and the receiver. There may be cases when your relationship with the receiver or your level of authority is such that you can persuade someone by saying "Just trust me on this," but these instances are rare.

Logical messages reflect relationships such as cause and effect that are objective in nature. Generally, people expect these relationships to be substantiated by some kind of evidence. If the school is commending its mathematics program in its marketing materials, people are more likely to be persuaded of its excellence if the message is supported by results data (evidence of higher student achievement in math).

To construct logical messages, use language and connections that people will understand. A good approach is to state the problem, describe the solution, and show the results in a descriptive way. If you can do this by telling a story or using a visual, the message is even more appealing.

In a presentation to show the effectiveness of a high school's program to decrease dropout rates, the narrator tells the story of one 16-year-old student. He describes the boy's problems in school, his feelings of alienation, poor grades, and his inability to find any reason to stay in school. Then the narrator explains how the high school's program of intervention through counseling, after-school activities, and mentoring kept the boy in school until he graduated. The story ends with the boy's enrollment in a 2-year associate degree program. The personal tone of the story combined with facts about the emotional, social, and economic costs of dropouts for the individual and the community makes a compelling argument for the high school's program.

Emotion. Emotion is a powerful persuader. Even though we believe it is unwise to make decisions when we are emotional, and we are critical of arguments that play on our emotions, as feeling human beings, we are nevertheless susceptible to emotional appeals. Individuals, even entire nations, have allowed emotion to prevail over logic. History is replete with heroic and villainous deeds spawned by the ability to manipulate people through emotional arguments. The lucrative nature of motivational seminars is an indication of the appeal of emotional public speaking.

Because emotional arguments are generally more persuasive than logical ones, advertisers spend much time and money determining the types of messages that will tap their audience's emotions. It is virtually impossible to develop a persuasive message that contains no emotional appeal. Even if I try to sell you toothpaste with a logical argument about how regular brushing with my product will protect against tooth decay and loss, I will attempt to capitalize on your fear of potentially painful, expensive dental treatments, and loss of teeth if you do not practice regular dental hygiene.

We often defend our emotional decisions with logic. If my ego and vanity influence me to spend a great sum of money for a luxury car, I may try to justify my action with a logical argument that the car is a better investment, will last longer, or is safer than a cheaper one.

Generating positive emotions is more persuasive than producing negative ones. Often it is simply phrasing that makes one message more effective than another. Saying, "Our students will be safer with new security systems and policies," is more effective than a negative, more frightening statement, "Without the implementation of new security systems and policies, students are in jeopardy."

Because emotional appeals are subjective, the persuasiveness of the message depends on the receiver more so than a logical argument. Gender, age, race, educational level, and other characteristics play a significant role in message reception. Knowing your audience is essential to creating effective emotional messages.

Use emotional appeals with a heavy dose of caution. Highly emotional arguments may work in the short run, but if they are baseless or heavy-handed, the result is a loss of credibility. There is a difference between creating legitimate concern and scaring people.

Credibility. Many people argue that the most important element in persuasive communication is the credibility of the source. The idea is that no matter how persuasively logical or emotional an argument is, if the receiver does not hold the source as credible, he will not be persuaded. Often messages that may have been ignored are given credence if the sender is perceived as trustworthy.

The receiver determines the credibility of the source. That is why someone listening to a politician from the party she supports is likely to find the argument highly persuasive while another person from an opposing side finds the same argument incredulous. Advertisers pay entertainers and sports figures large sums of money to promote their products because much of the public finds these figures credible whether they have reason to or not.

One of the first instances of such advertising occurred decades ago. An actor, Robert Young, extolled the "benefits" of drinking Sanka decaffeinated coffee in television commercials. Young had no reason to be more credible about the benefits of coffee than any other actor or person. His credibility came from his years as the compassionate Dr. Marcus Welby on a television series. Even though they knew he was not really a doctor, many viewers saw him as the caring, responsible doctor they knew from television who was always correct in his judgment. If Dr. Welby said Sanka was beneficial, it must be true. Advertisers quickly realized how effective this type of advertising is and have continued to make use of it.

The source of your school's communication should be appropriate to the message. Generally, we think of the principal as the appropriate source for communication, but in some cases teachers, counselors, or the school nurse may be more suitable.

In other situations, someone outside the school environment may have more credibility because she is seen as impartial. In some cases, alumni, parents, civic leaders, elected officials, volunteers, and business people may be perceived as more objective sources for communication than someone from the school, who may be perceived as self-serving. This is particularly true for issues involving public action or approval such as bond issues or tax increases. Often religious, ethnic, national, or cultural groups find someone who reflects the characteristics of their particular group more credible than someone outside the group. A poor student from the inner city who regularly deals with poverty, drugs, and violence may not be persuaded by advice from an older person from a privileged background.

Other factors that influence how credible a person is perceived are appearance, status, background, age, and context. Certain audiences may find a person in professional dress more credible than the one in casual dress. Unfair as it is, studies show that people are more easily persuaded by someone who is very attractive than one who is not. An article about the school or district in a nationally recognized newspaper may have more credibility than one in the neighborhood paper. Even the appeal of the person who introduces you before a speech may color the audience's perception of your credibility before you say a word.

Logic, emotion, and credibility should all be considered when constructing your messages. A good way to understand how these elements are used effectively is to analyze advertisements in magazines and on television. When an advertisement attracts or repels you, ask yourself why it does. Consider how logic, emotion, and credibility were used and why they were effective or ineffective in appealing to you. The marketing team can use this type of analysis as an exercise to help develop persuasive communication pieces.

LET YOUR AUDIENCE FILL IN THE BLANKS

Messages are particularly effective when they engage the audience in the reasoning process. This is accomplished by having the audience fill in the blanks, make connections, and come to the desired conclusions without explicit direction. The most effective way to accomplish this is through an interactive reasoning device known as an enthymeme. This may sound like a big, complicated word, but enthymemes are simply truncated or incomplete syllogisms. Remember the syllogism

All men are mortal
Socrates is a man
Therefore, Socrates is mortal

Enthymemes are similar to syllogisms except that the sender of the message omits either a premise or the conclusion with the expectation that the receiver will supply the appropriate missing element. If we take the Socrates syllogism mentioned above and omit either one of the premises or the conclusion, the expectation is that the receiver will complete the thought process in her own mind. Therefore, if I say, "All men are mortal and Socrates is a man," my expectation is that the receiver will conclude, "Oh, then Socrates must be mortal." Or, if I say, "Socrates is a man; therefore, he must be mortal," my expectation is that you will conclude, "All men must be mortal." The goal is to generate the most powerful kind of persuasion, self-persuasion.

One of the most extreme, famous, and controversial examples of the power of enthymemes was a political television advertisement created by Tony Schwartz. The advertisement known as the "Daisy" spot ran during the 1964 presidential race between Lyndon Johnson and Barry Goldwater.

The ad shows a little girl in a field trying to count as she pulls petals off a daisy. The audience hears her innocent voice saying, "1, 2, 3, 4, 5, 7, 6, 8, 9, 9." As she reaches "10," a strong male voice reverses the count, "10, 9, 8, 7, 6, 5, 4, 3, 2, 1." At zero, the freeze-frame on her face dissolves into deafening roar and the mushroom cloud of an atomic blast. The audience then hears the voice of Lyndon Johnson, "These are the stakes—to make a world in which all God's children can live, or to go into the darkness. We must either love each other, or we must die." As the advertisement fades, an authoritative voice says, "Vote for President Johnson on November 3. The stakes are too high to stay at home."

The advertisement neither mentions Johnson's Republican opponent, Barry Goldwater, nor connects him in any way with using a nuclear bomb. Senator Goldwater, however, was considered to be a "hawk" and he had made imprudent statements regarding using "nukes." Many who saw the commercial connected Goldwater's hawkish views with the chance that he might actually use the bomb, thereby obliterating millions of innocents like the little girl. However, the negative association of nuclear bombs and Goldwater was made *not* in the content of the commercial but in the minds of the people who viewed it. Individuals came to a conclusion that was not stated. The audience, in effect, self-persuaded.

The advertisement was so controversial it aired only once. However, the major networks reporting on the controversy showed the commercial on the evening news giving it free airtime and exposure to millions who had not seen it. The advertisement was devastating to Goldwater's election campaign.

Although the "Daisy" commercial used the enthymeme to make a negative association, they are just as powerful in making positive ones. During World War II, the government raised millions of dollars through war bonds by constructing messages built around the following premises:

Our country needs money to sustain the war effort.
War Bonds provide money.

The unspoken conclusion reached by those who read the messages and bought bonds was that by buying bonds they could help the country continue the war.

As simplistic as enthymemes may seem, they are powerful because receivers construct them in their own minds based on their own beliefs, attitudes, and values. For that same reason, they can backfire when the intended message of the omitted premise or conclusion is not one with which the receiver would agree. In the example of the war bonds above, the message was effective because most people in the United States believed that continuing the war was a right and necessary action. However, if the majority of people had been against the war, the message would have had an opposite effect.

In using enthymemes, consider the audience. Will they fill in the blanks and make the conclusions that you want them to? Remember, enthymemes are persuasive only when the message contains values, beliefs, and attitudes that are generally held by the audience.

The following examples show how enthymemes might be used in a school environment:

The text of the message is constructed around the following two premises:

Reading by the third grade is essential to success in later years
Our school's goal is for all students to read by the third grade
(conclusion)
Our school is working to ensure that our students will succeed in later years.

Or, the text might be constructed around these two premises:

Being able to read by the third grade is essential to student achievement in later years.
95 percent of our students can read by the third grade.
(conclusion)
95 percent of the school's students have an essential element for success in later years

When school administrators of a rural district became aware that a significant number of its students were not receiving proper dental care and that the lack of care was affecting the students' academic performance and social development, they initiated a project to improve dental health care for all children. Project participants included the dental community in a nearby town, PTO members, and county health-care professionals. The campaign to acquire donated goods and services wove the following premises into their messages:

Children in pain cannot learn.
Many children in the district are in pain from untreated tooth and gum disease.

(conclusion)
Many children are not learning because they lack dental care.

The project was successful in part because the premises upon which the appeal was based are generally held beliefs and attitudes. People abhor the idea of children being in pain, they know proper dental care is important, and they believe that all children should have the opportunity to learn.

With care and practice, the marketing team can begin to use enthymemes to create persuasive messages. It is always advisable to test the efficacy of your messages by asking individuals similar to your target audiences for their reactions and interpretations.

MAKING AN IMPRESSION

Sometimes we have only one opportunity to make a good impression. Have you ever had a disastrous job interview? You cannot call the next day and say, "I think I really made a mess of my interview. May I come back for another one?" People often form lasting impressions with minimal contact. The impression may be wrong, but an opportunity to correct it may not occur.

People in the community whether they are prospective parents, retired people, potential business partners, or community groups may form impressions of your school based solely on its communication materials. If the school newsletter is the only contact that an individual in the community has with the school, the quality of the writing, the content, and the appearance of the newsletter affect their impression of your school. If the brochure you send to prospective students and their parents is not persuasive, they may choose not to visit the school. If the proposal to potential business partners is not professional looking and well organized, they may not participate.

When I ask school administrators participating in my marketing workshops what they would most like to learn more about, creating effective marketing materials is in the top three (business partnerships and promotion activities are the other two). School administrators understand the need for well-designed materials, but are often dissatisfied with the results of their attempts.

It should be noted here that when I speak of marketing "materials" such as brochures, newsletters and other communication pieces, I include those that will be used in electronic mediums as well. A marketing piece may be either a hard copy or a digital version.

You may be fortunate enough to have a staff person already familiar with desktop publishing. If not, a number of excellent, user-friendly desktop publishing programs will allow you to produce quality brochures, newsletters, flyers, business cards, even posters for paper or electronic publishing with a minimum of learning time. I find Microsoft Publisher, Pro Publisher, and Corel Draw easy to use and I am not a techno-wizard.

Available publishing software should meet most of the school's needs. When the school wants a more complicated communication piece such as an annual report, a local print shop or graphics firm can help with layout, construction, graphics, and printing. Even if you use a professional firm to produce your communication pieces, you should have an idea of the overall look that you want and be able to provide the publisher with the content.

Much of the following content covers creating effective communication materials. Take the time to consider *all* elements of your communication pieces. A common mistake is not devoting enough time to the development of materials. Projects created in haste to meet a deadline are likely to prove disappointing. Always dedicate time to testing your communication pieces to avoid wasting resources on ineffective materials.

SOMETHING IS NOT ALWAYS BETTER THAN NOTHING

A well-designed school brochure can be an effective part of your marketing effort. However, schools often create brochures in haste because the feeling is, "We need to get something out there for people to see." It is better to have no brochure than to have one that is ineffective or creates negative reactions.

Use the following suggestions to help your team design a brochure, then solicit honest criticism from others including individuals outside your school environment. Especially important are members of any group that the brochure is targeting. This is not a time to let egos get in the way of effective communication. Consider suggestions and criticisms as useful information.

Avoid two common brochure mistakes. The first mistake is thinking that the brochure should focus on your school, your programs, your students, your achievements. The brochure should focus on *how what your school offers can benefit your audience*. Always keep your audience in mind as you create the brochure. Consider their needs, desires, language requirements, social values, economic and social status, and perceptions of your school.

The second mistake is thinking that a brochure is a silver bullet that will meet all marketing needs. I frequently encounter the notion that marketing consists mainly of creating and distributing brochures. Brochures are an important piece in your marketing effort. A well-designed brochure is an excellent introduction piece to persuade the reader to take further action in relation to your school. However, it is impossible for a brochure to carry the entire marketing effort.

Brochures reach a limited number of people who often read them a single time. Other methods of communication can provide greater range and frequency. Brochures are best used to create interest and give the readers a brief, but tempting message that makes them want to know more. It provides a way for someone to take your message with her.

Below are guidelines for creating an effective brochure. These are discussed in greater detail in this chapter. *These suggestions also apply to other communication materials which are covered in detail in other parts in this chapter:*

- Create an interesting cover
- Keep the reader moving through the brochure with headings, bullets, and graphics
- Use appropriate colors
- Concentrate on the benefits to the reader
- Tell the reader what you want him to do (call for details, visit our school, contact us) and how to do it (provide telephone numbers, list visiting days)
- Avoid excessive clip art
- Limit the number of fonts
- Keep imagery sharp and clear
- Group and set apart like kinds of information
- Reinforce your message with repetition

TEMPT READERS TO LOOK INSIDE

Imagine yourself standing in line at the grocery store. While you wait, a dozen magazines vie for your attention. Why do you pick out one over the others? Certainly, an interest in the focus of the magazine is a primary factor. But, generally there are several magazines with the same focus (current events, sports, food, celebrities). Chances are you selected one because the photographs and the titles of the articles suggested something of interest to you was inside. Have you ever bought a bottle of wine because you found the label or the name appealing? Or, chosen a restaurant simply because of the way it looked? Something about the outside enticed you to try what was inside.

For the same reason, the cover of the school's communications pieces greatly influences the decision to look inside. Indeed, the principal purpose of the cover is to create enough interest for someone to pick up the piece and read more. Picture your communication piece lying on a table surrounded by others that are competing for attention. Is there anything about it that would entice someone to select it over the others?

Color, images, and text contribute to an appealing cover. The colors should be appropriate (see the section on color in this chapter) and of good quality. Images should be relevant to the message and the reader. Text should have a succinct, inviting message that leads the reader to the next page.

Keep the text on the cover to a minimum. A brochure cover with too much text tires the reader before she gets to the first page. The lead-in text or headline on the cover can engage the reader when you . . .

- Say something unexpected
- Communicate a benefit
- Reinforce the school name
- Create curiosity
- Ask a question
- State a problem and give a solution
- Give a command
- Make a connection to the reader

Grab a
pencil
and

Sign up for
Summer School

June 7 - July 16, 2004
Riverside High School
999-123-4568

Figure 4.1   Use common objects in different ways.

Accompanying images can dramatically increase the appeal of your message but they should be relevant to the message and the reader. If you are creating a brochure for Spanish-speaking parents, most of the images should represent the group's ethnicity. Images should reinforce not detract from the message.

Too much clutter detracts from the message. Stay away from ornate images unless their ornate quality is relative to the message. If you want to use clip art of typical school images such as apples, books, schoolhouses, crayons, etc., use them in an innovative or imaginative fashion to make your cover stand out from the many others that have school-related objects. Figure 4.1 is an example of typical school objects used in a different way.

WIFM?

A common mistake in creating marketing materials is thinking that the focus should be on the school or district. Like other aspects of marketing, promotional materials should focus on the target audience.

Often I see school brochures that visually make a good impression with excellent photographs, nice layout, appealing colors, and informative text about the school's performance, standards, and programs. Everything assures me of the school's excellence. However, the one thing that would create an interest in the school is missing. Nothing in the brochure communicates how what the school offers would benefit *me*, the reader. *The WIFM (What's In It For Me) element is missing.*

There is a saying in marketing, "Customers don't want ¼ inch drill bits, customers want ¼ inch holes." The buyer is not interested in the product; he is interested in what the product can do for him. If a person has no interest in making ¼-inch holes, he will not be interested in ¼-inch drill bits no matter how great the advertising or the product is.

When people are presented with brochures, advertisements, or any other type of promotional material, there is one question going through their minds, "What's in it for me?" That is human nature.

I might become interested in ¼-inch drill bits if I feel that being able to make ¼-inch holes offers me benefits. The benefits may be logical or emotional, tangible or intangible. I might be convinced that being able to make ¼-inch holes would make my book shelf project faster and easier to complete (logical). I would feel self-reliant (emotional), because I could assemble a new book case myself (tangible). My friends would see me as a capable and clever person (intangible).

Do not assume that the reader will inevitability make the connection between what the school offers and the benefits. The benefit to the reader must be clear. One effective way to answer the WIFM question is to provide the reader with the connection between the features of your product and the derived benefits or rewards. To be most effective, the benefits should be specific and stated at the beginning to peak the reader's interest.

Below are examples of feature-based statements

Last year our school introduced an innovative reading program for all students.

(With no benefit attached, the likely response is, "So what?")

Good
Our school provides all students with an innovative reading program to improve their reading skills.

(This is better, but what is the specific benefit?)

Better
Our innovative reading program is helping students improve their reading skills as much as one level in six months.

(Now, a specific benefit is attached that clarifies the WIFM. But, to catch the reader's attention, state the benefit first.)

Best
Our students are improving their reading skills as much as one level in six months with our innovative reading program.

(Now, the first thing the reader sees is the benefit which will prompt him to continue reading.)

Here is another example:
This year our school has a new earth sciences program.

Good
Our new earth sciences program encourages children to see the world in new ways.

Better
Your child will see the earth in new ways with our new earth sciences program.

Best

Learning becomes exciting when your child sees the earth in new ways with our new earth sciences program.

A good way to write benefit-focused text is to imagine yourself as the likely recipient. What features would attract and hold your interest? What kind of benefits would be appealing? Does the text match your interests? Then ask someone who is typical of the intended receiver to critique your piece using those same questions to see if you got it right.

KEEP THE READER MOVING

The layout of your document can make it visually inviting or uninviting. No matter how interesting your copy is, if the document looks too wordy or cluttered, the reader may not even attempt to read it.

It is tempting to put as much information into the piece as possible. You want to tell the reader *everything*. The reader is not interested in everything your school has to offer at this point. It may be that the reader is not interested in anything your school has to offer at this point. The goal is to create interest and persuade the reader to want to know more. Long lines of text in the document in Figure 4.2 create the impression that there is a lot of information to read. And, there is nothing other than text to draw the reader's attention.

The text is more interesting and readable when it is broken up with images, color, headings, and space.

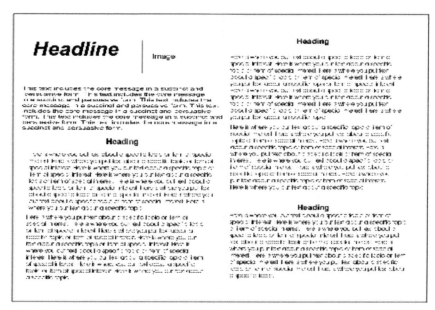

Figure 4.2   Large chunks of long lines of text may discourage someone from reading the message.

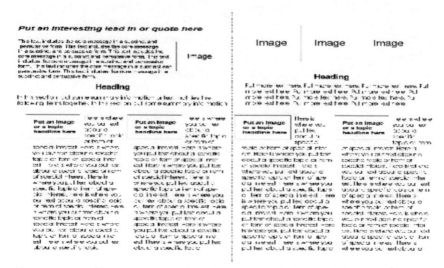

Figure 4.3   Breaking up the text and adding images makes the message more appealing.

- Keep the reader's eyes moving forward with headings, bullets, color, images, white space, and columns. Break text into manageable chunks and use bold headings to alert the reader to the content.
- A good ratio of text to white space is 60 percent text, 40 percent white space. Take care not to create large gaps of white space between chunks of text or other elements in your design. This interrupts the movement of the reader's eyes through the document.
- Use lists, such as,
  10 Reasons why . . .
  4 things that most . . .,
  5 steps to . . . .
- Use bullets and short lines of text to list items.

The layout in Figure 4.3 is a more inviting design.

GIVE AUDIENCES A REASON TO TAKE ACTION, THEN TELL THEM HOW

Even though people find your message persuasive, they may need encouragement to follow through on it.

The typical text below may generate some action:

Register for the fine arts program before May 15th by completing and returning the enclosed form or visiting our website.

However, more reader-oriented text with specific information will get a better response.

To ensure your child has an exciting range of fine arts programs this summer, complete the enclosed registration form and return it to your child's teacher or register online at arts@lincolnms.org *before May 15th.*

If you want readers to do something such as visit the school, call for more information, check your website, follow the school on Facebook or Twitter, or register early, it is important to tell them exactly how. If you want people to visit the school, you need to tell them when they can visit (dates or days and hours). If they need to arrange the visit in advance, tell them with whom to make an appointment and how. Give directions to the school and tell them where to go when they get there.

It is human nature to find an excuse not to do something even when we think we should. Motivate your audience to take action by giving them a reason why they should, then make it easy for them to follow through.

IMAGERY CREATES INTEREST

Photographs are as important as headlines and text. People like to look at pictures. An interesting photograph is often the reason someone chooses to read an article, newsletter, or a brochure. A photograph will draw attention to an item and a good photograph will draw the reader into the text.

Digital photography and the high-quality reproductions from affordable photocopiers and printers make including photographs in your communication pieces easy and cost-effective. However, the best cameras, copiers, and printers cannot improve a photograph that is technically inferior.

A photograph that is out of focus, blurred, or over- or underexposed is unacceptable no matter how interesting the subject or composition. Quality photographs require good equipment; but good equipment does not have to be the best or the most expensive. Quality equipment is available at reasonable costs. High-quality photographs can now be made with most mobile phones. Digital cameras and mobile phones provide ways to improve your photographs on the spot.

Composition, the arrangement of people and objects in the picture, creates visual appeal. For many people, composition is the most difficult aspect of photography because it requires changing many of our old habits such as taking full body shots of everyone facing forward and looking at the camera.

Photographs should be relevant and interesting. They should provide visible support or explanation for the main message of your communication

Examples of good photographic elements.

piece. If you are writing an article for the local paper about the new buses that can carry disabled students, a picture of a student being lifted into the bus is more interesting than a picture of just the bus.

Below are some ways to create interesting photographs.

- Use contrast. A photograph with shadows or silhouettes against a light background or light figures against a dark background is better than one in which nothing stands out. Contrast also draws the eye to the photograph. If you have a camera with a viewfinder that allows you to bring the background or foreground into sharper focus you can concentrate attention on a specific element by blurring the surrounding area.
- Use action. I am amazed at the constancy with which people are lined up like bowling pins for photographs. My first reaction is that the related story will probably be as boring as the picture. People *do things* when they are at meetings, events, or school functions. Capture people doing something in your photographs even if it is just standing and talking with each other. A typical graduation photo is the valedictorian giving her speech. It is understandable that you want to give the valedictorian recognition, but also include photographs of students hugging each other or a family weeping with pride. A good photograph captures the essence of what is happening.
- Use different angles. You can improve the most mundane photograph with different camera angles. Rather than shooting your picture head on, kneel and shoot up, stand at a higher elevation and shoot down, or shoot a side shot to create a different perspective. Consider the traditional groundbreaking photograph of dignitaries in hard hats lined up with their shovels. A more interesting picture would be one taken from a kneeling position that shows the dirt flying with the dignitaries in the background. An interesting photographic angle conveys the idea the related story may also have an interesting angle.
- Use imagination. Come up with interesting ways to get your message across by indulging in atypical thinking. A typical way to photograph the new pottery-making equipment for the creative arts class would be to show the students and teacher in a group gazing proudly at the new equipment. A more interesting photograph would be a close-up shot of a student as he spins a mound of clay on the potter's wheel or a student admiring the result of her first attempt at pottery-making. The mixed emotions that many students and parents feel on a child's first day of school might be captured by a close-up of parent and child saying good-bye. Do not be afraid to try new and different approaches. No one has to see the ideas that did not work, but you can learn from them.
- Use fewer not more. Unless there is a specific reason for having a large number of people in a picture, avoid large groups. A close-up picture of

one band member pounding on his large drum is more interesting than the whole band marching down the street. The general rule is no more than five people in a picture. Also keep in mind that odd numbers of objects or people are always more visually interesting than even numbers. One, three, or five people create a more interesting picture than two, four, or six.

- Take lots of photos. One way to get good pictures is to take many of them. I once attended a photography course taught by a freelance photographer who had worked on *National Geographic* assignments. For an article that included seven or eight photographs he would shoot around 100 rolls of film! He did not suggest that we, as amateur photographers, do the same; his point was that getting a good photograph requires taking more than two or three pictures. Taking more than just a few shots also encourages you to be more creative and adventuresome. A big advantage of digital cameras is that they allow you to take many pictures, see them instantly, and discard the rejects.
- Use new technology. New software now allows you to do many things with your computer that before required expertise in a darkroom. You can improve photographs by cropping, increasing the contrast, correcting lighting, and using other enhancing capabilities. Even your mobile phone will allow you to edit photographs!
- Use naturalness. One way to achieve naturalness in your photos is to take pictures without your subjects being aware. People have an inclination to stop and stare at the camera when they realize they are being photographed. If people stop to "pose," simply put down your camera and ask them to continue with their activities or, at least, not to stare at the camera.
- Use children. Too many school-related photographs are of school officials or other adults. Children are natural attention getters. The uninhibited, spontaneous nature of children will produce far more interesting pictures than a group of administrators. In a groundbreaking event, why not take a picture of a few children with hard hats and shovels instead of administrators? The education of children is why schools exist; it is only natural that they be the focus of your photographs. One caveat, be sure to get signed permission from parents or guardians to reproduce and use photographs.

THE LANGUAGE OF COLOR

First impressions are often lasting impressions. According to the Institute for Color Research, the average person forms an impression within 90 seconds and between 63 percent and 90 percent of their impression is based on color.

Male birds are brightly colored for a reason. They need to stand out from the competition and catch the attention of females. Humans, too, are attracted by color, but as thinking beings, we attach meaning to color.

We are attracted to color from the moment we begin to distinguish objects. Babies and young children are attracted to bright colors before they are attracted to specific objects. Our color preferences may change as we grow older, but we remain influenced by color. Color becomes a way to make a statement about ourselves. I am fun. I am traditional. I am rebellious.

Colors can change from being "in" to being "out." Red is in this year, gray is out. You may be old enough to remember "avocado" appliances. Even the "always appropriate" little black dress occasionally falls from favor. Avoid trendy colors when designing logos or promotional materials that you intend to keep for a time; otherwise, you may be "out" next year.

Colors can send messages that are stronger than the words used. Black balloons with the words *"Happy Birthday"* send a message that this is a birthday the recipient may not be "happy" to celebrate. A color that is not appropriate for the message generates a sense of irony.

Much of our reaction to color is subconscious; therefore, we are often unaware of how colors affect us. But, corporations have been using color for decades in their advertising, packaging, corporate logos, and communication pieces to attract and persuade consumers.

To be effective, colors must be in harmony with the product and the message. Red and black packaging is as inappropriate for a bath product that claims to sooth and calm as are pastel colors for a gasoline additive that claims to add power to your engine. Expensive products call for colors that indicate the worth of the contents. A bargain calls attention to its low price with showy colors.

Although many reactions to colors are universal (red always attracts attention), some are culturally specific. The traditional Chinese bride wears red, a color symbolizing great luck. White, the color traditionally worn by Western brides, is a color of mourning for the Chinese. A look at the arts and crafts of a culture can give clues to which colors are significant and what they symbolize. For example, Native Americans favor earth tones indicative of nature, a dominant force in their culture. It is always wise to be aware of the feelings toward specific colors of cultural groups within your schools or district.

Below are traditional Western meanings associated with colors to consider when creating communication pieces.

- Red—conveys excitement, passion, and activity. It is virtually impossible to ignore red. Because it grabs our attention, bright red is good for accents and important words or statements. STOP signs are red for a reason. Dark red, like most dark, intense colors, suggests richness and expense. We refer to dark, intense colors by the expensive jewels we associate with them; ruby red, emerald green, sapphire blue. However, be careful when using red for it is also associated with debt, anger, and danger.

- Pink—suggests femininity, innocence, and youth. Pale pink conjures up a feeling of softness and sweetness. Good health is associated with pink. We say, *in the pink*, to mean being in a healthy state. Tones of pink might be used in a communication piece for a program on health issues for girls or a woman's exercise class offered after-hours at the school. However, pink is not a forceful color so it is not appropriate for urgent or critical messages.

- Orange—suggests fun, energy, and exuberance. It is a loud color better used in small measure to highlight or create a sense of liveliness. Avoid using bright shades of orange in situations where you want to be serious such as the school's annual report. Lighter shades, such as peach, apricot, or coral, are warm and appealing and can be used to offset more somber tones.

- Yellow—is associated with the sun, warmth, and energy in almost every culture. Like red, yellow is hard to ignore. The most visible car on the road is a yellow one. That is why a Yellow Cab is easier to see than a blue, white, even a red one. Pale shades of yellow appeal to our intellectual side. Pale cream colors are more elegant than white. High contrast and associated meanings make black and yellow one of the most powerful color combinations. Although a wonderful accent color, too much yellow can be harsh and annoying.

- Green—offers a wide array of choices with a variety of meanings. The abundance of green in nature creates an association with freshness and tranquility. Vibrant, eye-catching lime green colors are good as accents. Bright green symbolizes the new life and the sense of renewal that appears in the spring in the form of buds and grass. Pale tones of green are soothing. Dark green suggests status and money. There are also negative associations with green, being "green" with envy or turning "green" when sick.

- Blue—is a universally popular color that symbolizes authority, dignity, trustworthiness, and dependability. No wonder it is popular for designing corporate logos, especially those of financial institutions. Whereas bright, electric blue is dramatic and energizing, pale blue is a restful color that humans find calming; something to keep in mind if you have news that could agitate people. Dark blue connotes power and authority. That is why it is a popular color for uniforms. Teal blue is a sophisticated, distinctive, chic color that is equally appealing to men and women.

- Purple—is often overlooked as a color choice. Associated with royalty (we even call it royal purple), deep purple connotes a sense of gentility, tradition, and sensitivity. Purple also evokes feelings of spiritualism and sensuality that create strong reactions. Purple is good for sophisticated, artistic messages.

- Brown—is the ultimate earth tone. Brown gives the sense that something is solid, steady, dependable. Depending on the context, brown can be drab or rich. Out of favor for some time, the use of brown is now more widespread with the popularity of coffee bars, upscale brown leather furniture, and vans that come with packages for us. Such trends have an influence on how we react to colors. Using brown with an array of medium and lighter earth colors produces a look that is sophisticated without being pretentious and practical without being dull.

- Gray—is a serious, but sophisticated color with a wide variety of shades from deep charcoal to soft pale tones. Gray can be warm or cool. Gray tones down bright colors when the desire is to have brightness without being gaudy. Conversely, touches of bright colors and pastels lessen the drabness when gray is a predominate color. A gray suit with a dark red or yellow tie is a popular combination among executives; the message is, I am serious without being dull.

- Black—has evolved from its traditional association with death and darkness to become a color that creates a powerful, mysterious, dramatic, elegant, and expensive aura. Who would have thought thirty years ago that black kitchen appliances would be chic. Black tie, little black dress, black limousine, black leather, and black granite represent high style and success. Black in combination with other colors is especially powerful, but take care to ensure that the effect is not harsh and excessive.

- White—is associated with purity and cleanliness; however, white can also represent coldness and sterility. Creamy or off-white tones moderate the starkness of pure white. But, if you want to create a sense of freshness, crispness, and clarity, white is the color. White is the perfect background color, especially in contrast with more dramatic, bold colors. Black and white, the ultimate contrast, can produce dramatic results.

When choosing colors, consider how the colors work with each other to produce an effect. Combinations of colors can produce an instantaneous meaning, trigger a response, or set a mood for your message. Select colors in harmony with your message. Studies have shown that using colors inconsistent with your message generally generates negative responses. Black and orange for Christmas or red and green for Halloween will get attention, but not the kind you want.

Earthy colors such as orange, gold, dark green, brown, black, and deep red represent autumn, the rural countryside, and abundance associated with harvest. Use them in seasonal messages or messages that speak of down-to-earth values.

Festive colors such as bright pink, yellow, red, orange, bright green, and sky blue represent fun and gaiety. Use them to announce parties and events or energize people into action.

Serene or tranquil colors such as tones of deep blue, aqua, pale green, and lavender represent the sea and sky. Use them in messages to suggest tranquility, unity, or where a calming influence is required.

Combining black with colors such as yellow, purple, red, or gold creates dramatic, powerful combinations that should be used sparingly. If you constantly speak in a loud voice, you lose the impact of a shout. Use dramatic combinations only for your most important messages.

Experiment with color. Go to a paint store that provides large, single paint samples and collect some for use at your school. Arrange the colors in various combinations and ask for people's reactions. Most publishing software allows you to change colors easily, even on clip art, so you can test various combinations.

Color makes things come alive. It was exciting when people could exchange the old black- and-white television for a color one. Color is an important factor in how people act and react. Use it to your advantage.

REPETITION CREATES UNITY

Repetition of visual elements, such as colors, fonts, shapes, space, and other design elements, creates unity and consistency within your communication piece. Consistency is important if the piece is a prospectus or presentation booklet that comprises several pages. If each page has a different look, the message appears disjointed. If each page has a different design layout, the harmony is broken as the pages compete with each other. If you use a repetitive design or graphic throughout the piece, be sure that it is always in the same size, same place, same color, etc., unless there is a reason to deviate.

A common error is using too many fonts. Any variation in a font is considered a different font. Therefore, these fonts, **fonts**, *fonts*, fonts, fonts, are different even though they are all "Century" font. Limit the number of fonts to no more than two or three.

Even seemingly small items such as inconsistent margins and indents can create a disorganized impression. You want the reader to concentrate on the message, not be distracted by inconsistencies.

CONTRAST CREATES INTEREST

Contrast gets attention and creates interest. The same elements such as color, fonts, and space that create consistency can also produce contrast. White on black, light against dark, contrasting fonts, tight text in a large amount of white space, and an extra-large capital letter before smaller text will attract the eye to the message.

Excellence is *cool*

Don't Be a Bully

A is a beautiful grade

Some documents, such as policy statements, call for a minimalist look; but, even pages filled mostly with text can be more interesting when the font sizes of titles and subtitles are larger than the text in the body.

As with repetition, contrasts can be overdone. Whereas the overuse of repetition can be boring, overuse of contrast can be annoying.

REPEAT YOUR MESSAGE IN MULTIPLE WAYS

You want your readers to remember the key points of your message. Repetition of your message with photographs, graphs, quotes, and words can improve the chances the reader will retain key points. If the message is that a new curriculum is improving test scores, show a graph representing the improved scores over time, a quote from a teacher, or a photograph of a student proudly holding a paper with an "A." Elements, such as a picture, graph, or quote, often stay with the reader longer than lines of text.

You can reinforce your message by saying the same thing in different ways. To reinforce the message of better test results, you might refer to "improved test scores," "increased performance," and "we watched our test scores rise," throughout your piece. Take care, however, not to overdo it.

COLLECT THE GOOD, THE BAD, AND THE UGLY

Creative people get their ideas and inspiration from the world around them including other people's work. When you see an advertisement, poster, book cover, menu, newsletter, website, or anything that makes a strong impression on you, good or bad, take a photo of it with your phone and keep a copy of it and attach a note describing how you responded to it and why.

Ask each marketing team member to keep a file of samples they have gathered with notes on why they found them appealing or unappealing. Review the pieces periodically with the marketing team. Dissect the elements to decide why they were effective or ineffective. Were the colors annoying? Did the lead-in catch team members' attention and entice them to read further? Was the overall tone of the piece sophisticated, whimsical, impressive, irritating, or boring? What elements created specific impressions? When the marketing team is ready to design a new communication piece, review the samples to look for ideas.

TAGLINES AND SLOGANS

Have you ever found yourself using an advertising slogan as part of your everyday speech? "Where's the beef?," "When it rains, it pours," and "Just do it!" are examples of slogans that became a part of our conversation. Some slogans last for years, others for a few months.

The purpose of a slogan is to create a conscious or unconscious connection to and awareness of a product or service. To attract attention and help with retention, advertisers use devices such as rhyme, alliteration, puns, and metaphors. Slogans may ask a question, give a command, or make a promise. If the slogan creates a positive feeling toward the product or organization then it has served its purpose.

Schools and districts can use slogans to create an identity, promote a campaign, advertise a program, recruit teachers, or establish a position. Below are examples of school-related slogans.

Command: *Watch us achieve*
Personification: *A learning environment that embraces all students*
Hyperbole: *Our science program knows no earthly bounds*
Inversion: *Common sense. Uncommon results*
Question: *Will YOU be my teacher?*
Alliteration: *Creating creative classrooms*
Metaphor: *A bridge between thinking and doing*
Puns: *We attract talent* (a fine arts magnet school) or
A magnet for inquisitive minds (a science magnet school)
School or mascot name: Teaching our *Eagles* to soar
Repetition: *We can, We do, We will succeed*

If you decide that using a slogan or tagline is appropriate for your school, district, or program, below are some tips for creating one:

- Use one or more brainstorming sessions to generate ideas.
- Before your brainstorming session, ask the participants to collect slogans and taglines they like.
- Ask for ideas from school staff members and students.
- In your session, review the collected slogans and discuss why they are appealing.
- Write down as many words or phrases as you can that explain exactly what the school does. What are its attributes? How is the school different? What are its goals?
- Look for words or phrases that come to mind most often.
- Try to make your tagline as specific to your school or district as possible.
- Avoid worn-out phrases (committed to excellence, standard of quality).
- Unless you can be extraordinarily clever, avoid tying your slogan to current, trendy advertising slogans. When the slogan is no longer trendy, yours will sound dated. Moreover, there could be legal consequences if copyrights exist.

After you have come up with several possibilities, try them out on people inside and outside the school. Take a poll among students and staff members. Strive for a slogan that people feel proud to use and follow.

CREATING A LOGO

One of the charming attractions of medieval cities in Europe is the array of symbols and images hanging over the doorways of commercial establishments to designate the various trades and merchants. Many of these icons came to represent a standard of excellence that has been treasured and protected over centuries. These symbols were precursors to our present-day logos.

A logo is an image that represents an organization and the product or service it provides. A logo may be an image, like the Mercedes emblem or the Nike swoop, distinctive lettering such as Coca Cola's red script, or a combination of both such as the image of Colonel Saunders combined with Kentucky Fried Chicken. Some logos, such as Coca Cola's distinctive red lettering and McDonalds' golden arches, are so well known worldwide they symbolize American culture as well as the products they represent. Logos are powerful reminders of the attributes of an organization. Like companies, schools can benefit from a well-designed logo.

To be effective, your logo should be attractive, distinctive, and memorable. Being attractive does not mean just looking good; it means attracting attention in a positive way. An attractive image draws the eye to it and holds attention even if for a second or two. Being distinctive requires that it stand out from other similar types of logos. If your logo looks like every other school logo, the message is that your school is like every other school. When people see it, you want them to think of *your* school, not *a* school. A memorable logo is one that leaves an impression so that the next time the viewer sees it, there is recognition.

Most logos comprise three elements: a graphic, lettering or wording, and color. The McDonald's logo consists of two arches, the name McDonald's and the predominant color, yellow. There are exceptions. Some logos are so recognizable, no wording is needed, the Red Cross for example. Some logos are simply the organization's name in a consistent design, for example, Coca Cola.

The school logo should be simple, attractive, and compatible with the school's purpose. If the school is creating a completely new logo, start with the three elements of graphic, color, and font, then refine the design. If the school has designated colors, use them or use the color guide (discussed earlier) to select colors in keeping with the image and message the school wants to communicate.

Think about how your logo will look in all sizes, small on a shirt pocket or large on a 10-foot banner. Use a font that is readable even when the logo is reduced in size. Some fonts become illegible in smaller sizes. Create a graphic that is clean and distinctive. All three elements should blend well. An ornate graphic with stark, ultra-sleek lettering is likely to create a conflict that is disagreeable to the viewer. However, there are no hard and fast rules. Doing something out of the ordinary sometimes results in a truly distinctive design.

A contest to design a school logo could generate excellent designs. Moreover, a logo is more meaningful if it is created from within the school. Write a brief history of logo design with well-known examples (information is available on the Internet), establish guidelines for the design, and then hold a contest. Encourage everyone, staff members, teachers, and students, to participate. Create a selection committee to pick the best one or select four or five of the best designs and hold a school-wide selection. After a design has been selected or voted on, hold an official "unveiling."

Once the school has gone to the effort to create a logo, use it. Put the logo on all school communications, decals for notebooks, school banners, uniforms, give-away items, and any other promotional materials. The logo should be a recognizable, positive symbol of the school.

Remember to copyright the logo. If the school comes up with an outstanding design that is getting attention, you do not want some other organization or school to copy it. Information on the process and requirements of copyrights is available on the Internet.

ANNUAL REPORTS

A school's annual report is most effective when it tells the audience clearly and concisely what *they* want to know about the school. Because a school's annual report can also serve as a prospectus to recruit students and teachers, solicit funds and community support, and report the state of the school or district to its constituents, it should be professional in appearance and content. The cover should be simple and appealing and communicate that the contents are important. If the school has specific colors, use them; otherwise, select colors that reflect a desired image of the school.

Some of the items to include in an annual report are:

- A letter from the superintendent or principal providing a summary of the year
- The district's or school's position and vision statements
- A history including important events, awards, special achievements and distinctions, and distinguished alumni
- A directory of administrators and contact information
- Description of special programs including extracurricular activities
- Student/teacher ratios
- Numerical and graphical account of student performance
- Graduation rates
- Percentage of students pursuing higher education after graduation
- Student demographic information
- School physical environment (condition of school, level of technology, special facilities)
- Safety record
- PTO activities
  - Parental support
  - Educational levels of teaching and administrative staff
  - Grants awarded to the school
- Community involvement including external partnerships and volunteer programs

The first annual report will require the most work. Spend sufficient time and money to create layout and design features that the school will want to replicate year after year. It may be worth the money to hire a graphic designer to help with the design. After the first year, the work will involve revising data in the existing report. I suggest that the school change the cover design in some way each year. It differentiates the reports and coveys the idea that the contents are current. To cut down on costs, print a limited number and make the report available online.

TESTIMONIALS ARE MARKETING GOLD

An advertisement for a new restaurant in your neighborhood may or may not persuade you to try it. However, if your neighbor tells you she tried the restaurant and the food, service, and atmosphere were superb and the prices were reasonable, then the chances are high that you will try it. Why? Because your neighbor has nothing to gain from her praise of the restaurant. Her recommendation is unbiased; therefore, it is more credible than an advertisement. You feel assured that if you try the restaurant you will not be disappointed. Her recommendation reduced the risk.

Testimonials are powerful persuaders and should be included in your marketing communication. People expect the school to sing its own praises; it is different when someone without a vested interest sings them. The marketing strategy of the infomercial is to break down the resistance people have toward a sales person by having product users tell the audience how great the product is.

Testimonials are most effective when they are specific and personal such as a parent explaining how a school program specifically met his child's needs or a high school student relating how a program is preparing her for college. Alumni can provide persuasive testimonials when they describe how a teacher or the school environment was a factor in their achievements later in life. Keep the testimonials brief, no more than three or four lines unless you are using a story as a testimonial. Do not limit testimonials to written statements. Being able to hear and see someone on a video is particularly effective.

Once you have testimonials, use them. Include testimonials in distributed materials such as brochures and the annual report, post them on the school website, or put them on a poster. Include taped testimonials in a school or district video. An ambitious, but meaningful project would be to create a testimonial calendar. Each month include a picture of students, teachers, parents, or alumni involved in a school-related activity with an accompanying testimonial. For instance, a picture of children involved in a science project would include a testimonial from an alumna about how Mr. Simon's science class was the beginning of her path to becoming a doctor.

Testimonials add credibility to your message. They also generate loyalty. When people really believe in a product, they want to help it succeed. A testimonial is a way for supporters to feel they are playing a part in the school's success.

FAX MORE THAN JUST A COVER SHEET

Although faxing documents is not as common as it used to be, people still use fax machines. Your school's fax cover sheet can be more than just a transmittal form. Use the cover sheet as a vehicle to market your school by

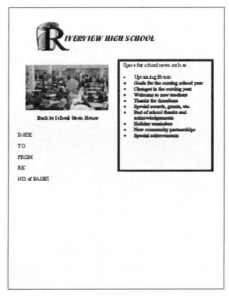

Figure 4.4   Fax sheet example.

communicating positive information to everyone who receives a fax. Include text boxes and photographs to share good news items; acknowledge students, employees, volunteers, and business partners; publicize your achievements; issue reminders; and promote upcoming events (see Figure 4.4 for an example). Update it monthly to keep recipients interested in its content.

NEWSLETTERS SHOULD BE NEWSY

Everyone in your community should be aware of your school's or district's accomplishments, its value to the community, and the important issues related to education. Within the first few months of moving into a new house, I received a district newsletter from the school district where I lived, and I continued to receive one each semester. Even though I no longer had children in public schools, I am a taxpayer and the school district believed I should be informed about the value received for my tax dollars.

Newsletters sent to your community are a way to maintain an awareness of your existence and to keep open a positive line of communication. To be effective, a newsletter should be:

• Informative. If the reader does not find any "new" news, why should he read it? The purpose of the newsletter is to provide information that the reader is not likely to have, but would like to have.

- Current. An invitation to an event that happened days before the newsletter arrives is of no use.
- Inclusive. Include news that covers the interests of a wide range of readers. News about the upcoming bond referendum or school board meeting may be of interest even to those without children in school.
- Interesting. Use photographs and headlines that will pique the reader's interest, then write text that will hold it.
- Visually attractive. Use layout, color, white space, and fonts to create an overall effect that looks appealing.
- Readable. Avoid jargon, acronyms, educational theories, and complicated statistics unless there is a reason for them and you explain them simply and thoroughly.

Put newsletters in the waiting areas of businesses. Doctor's or dentist's offices, tire or auto repair services, banks, or veterinarians provide an opportunity to get positive news about what the school is doing to people in the community who may not otherwise know. You never know who might pick up one of your newsletters and become interested in volunteering, enrolling a child, or becoming a business partner.

Your publications reflect the standards of your school so be sure that they are well done and interesting. Have article titles that are likely to catch someone's interest. Include "thank you's" to the school's partners, recognize volunteers, and give readers an easy way to contact the school and learn more about special programs and activities.

ARE YOU SURE THEY ARE READING IT?

When I was in public relations in the private sector, our firm conducted a special member promotion for a new client, a large credit union. To save money, the credit union asked us to enclose the promotion announcement in the monthly member newsletter. When we asked our clients if they were certain that most of the members read the newsletter, they exclaimed, "Of course! Our members love our newsletter." The promotion announcement was sent to approximately 7,000 members. The newsletter requested that the members call my firm's office to indicate their interest in participating in the promotion. We had extra staff ready to handle the calls.

The first week we received a small number of calls. The next week, a few more calls came in. We could not understand why response was so low. The client was very disappointed. The third week, we began to get calls that sounded something like this, "A friend of mine told me that he had heard from a friend of his about a great promotion that was available to credit union members. He gave me this number to call. What is the promotion and why were we not told about it?" When we explained that a promotion announcement had been included in the member newsletter, the usual response was, "Oh, I never read the newsletter." The credit union had never asked its members if the newsletter was meeting their needs and wants. They assumed members were reading it, because members never complained about it.

To ensure that the newsletter is meeting the recipients' needs, conduct a reader survey occasionally. The school newsletter is an opportunity to communicate with individuals with whom the school has no other direct contact. A brief newsletter survey can keep your school in touch with the needs and

Lincoln Middle School

3478 Elm Avenue
Houston, Texas 77019

We believe it is important to keep our community informed about what is happening in their school. One way we do this is through our Lincoln Middle School Newsletter. You can tell us how well we are meeting your information needs by completing this brief newsletter survey. We thank you for your time and look forward to seeing you at the next school event.

1. The newsletter is sent monthly. How often do you receive it?
    Every time   Occasionally   Never

2. How often do you read the newsletter?
    Always   Often   Occasionally   Never

3. How much of the newsletter do you read?
    All of it   Most of it   Some of it

4. How would you describe the overall look of the newsletter?
    Very good   Good   Fair   Poor

5. How would you describe the content of the newsletter?
    Very good   Good   Fair   Poor

6. Please list any kind of information you would like to see in the newsletter that is not presently in it.

7. Please list any suggestions you have for improving the newsletter on the reverse side.

Figure 4.5   Sample newsletter survey.

wants of your community. Figure 4.5 is a sample of a newsletter survey you can modify to meet your school's needs. Print the school's address on the reverse side so that other respondents can fold the survey and mail it.

BE "PRESENTABLE" IN THE COMMUNITY

One of the best ways to promote your school effectively is to get out into the community and talk about it. Having a speakers' bureau of individuals who are willing and prepared to make presentations about school achievements and issues promotes proactive communication and builds community relationships. Presentations can be used to provide general information or address specific issues of interest to people. Administrators and other school personnel often avoid this effective communication tool due to a lack of confidence in how to create and deliver a successful presentation. Following are a few rules which will improve presentation skills.

- Be organized. Outline your presentation in a logical sequence that will help the audience follow the material and remember it. Follow the old format of telling them what you are going to say, say it, then tell them what you said. That gets your point across three times.

  Begin with something that will grab the audience's attention. It does not have to be a joke. It could be a story, a question, a quotation, an unusual statement or statistic, or a bit of history. "Last week a student came to my office with a story that I found shocking and I think you will too." "How would you feel if . . .?" "Would you be surprised to know that . . .?"

  To illustrate your central points, you can start with a general statement or idea and then provide details to support your thesis or you can use details to build to a general conclusion. You might begin with a brief history of an issue and end with what you see in the future. However you structure your presentation, the audience should be able to see the logic of it.

- Be brief. The old saying, 'Leave them laughing," has merit. It is better to end your presentation while your audience still finds it interesting than talk so long that they wish you would stop. Even those who are interested will find themselves tuning out if your presentation is too long. Generally 20 minutes is a good length.

  Stories are a great way to illustrate a point, create emotion, or inject some humor, but keep them short. A general rule is to keep them under two minutes. Too many details and extraneous descriptions can detract from the point. In addition, the story should have a point. To ensure brevity, limit the story to describing *who, what, when, where, how, and why.*

Leave some time for question and answers. This is an opportunity to provide specific information and to gain insight into what is of interest to the audience. Offer interested individuals ways to find out more about your subject such as the school website, a brochure or pamphlet, a call or visit to the school.

- Do not read to your audience. A big part of being a successful speaker is personal interaction with the audience. When a speaker hunches over a lectern to read from a sheaf of papers, interaction is virtually nil and the result is audience boredom.

Generally, people read to their audiences because they are afraid they will forget what to say, stray off the message, or stumble over words. One of the best confidence builders is practice. Record your presentation on a CD and practice in your car. Stand in front of a mirror and practice looking relaxed and confident as you speak. Practice in front of your cat. Keep practicing until you feel confident. Practicing will reinforce the content and help you with your tempo.

It is okay to use notes or an outline to keep yourself on track and jog your memory. Another way to give yourself prompts and provide visuals for the audience is with presentation software such as PowerPoint. Do not give into the temptation, however, to fill your presentation slides with text and read from them.

Of course, the best practice is speaking before an audience. The more public speaking you do, the easier and more enjoyable it becomes. When you have exciting and important things to say about your school and feel confident in your ability to communicate with your audience, you will look for opportunities to speak.

- Expect the unexpected. Do not assume that everything you need for your presentation will be available for you even if you have been told it will be. Experience has taught me to carry my own equipment. Laptops, lightweight projectors, and portable, freestanding flipcharts that can sit on a table make being prepared easy.

Be prepared to give a shorter version of your presentation. If there is a speaker before you who runs over into your time space, ask if the group would prefer a shorter version of your presentation. Having a shorter version is better than trying to rush through your presentation. If the group is on a strict time schedule, they will appreciate your consideration and your adaptability.

Assume that there will be questions about points in your presentation. Be prepared to back up your line of reasoning. Have sources for any quotations, statistics, or data that you provide, think of questions that could arise, and anticipate challenges to your argument. Being able to meet objections and answer questions gives credibility to your presentation.

- Include internal experts. School administrators are the obvious choice to make presentations, but do not overlook individuals with special knowledge or experience. Teachers, students, parents, and volunteers can be effective speakers for the school.

  School staff members who have first-hand knowledge of the subject are particularly convincing to audiences. Students demonstrating the science project that won an award or a counselor explaining what the school is doing to address the causes of violent student behavior can be more compelling than hearing it from the principal. Curriculum experts can help with presentations on new state testing standards or a new curriculum. The district health professional can bring credibility to a presentation on how the schools are working with local agencies to handle an unexpected flu epidemic.

  Presentations can include more than one person. Trying to carry the entire presentation on a subject about which you feel apprehensive can elevate your anxiety level and affect your performance. The audience will understand and appreciate the inclusion of additional speakers who have special knowledge and experience.
- Use visuals sparingly. I once saw a cartoon in the New Yorker magazine in which Satan is sitting at his desk in his office in Hell interviewing a devilish looking job applicant. Satan is saying to the applicant, "I need someone who is an expert in torture. Do you know PowerPoint?" The cartoon illustrates the misuse and overuse of PowerPoint that has made this excellent presentation medium a torture for many people.

  PowerPoint made it easy for those of us who cannot write a straight line on a flip chart, have a tendency to wander off the topic, or need memory prompts when speaking. It also relieved us of the need to make and keep track of transparencies and charts. However, many succumbed to the temptation of letting it carry the weight of the presentation.

  PowerPoint is so visually appealing and easy to use that instead of being a visual enhancement for a presentation, PowerPoint slides often become a substitute for the presentation. Slides are filled with text. Now, instead of watching the presenter read from pages of text, the audience is subjected to watching him read from dozens of slides. Avoid turning your PowerPoint presentation into wall size note cards.

  Charts, pictures, or other visuals can help the audience "see" the points you are making; however, too many can be distracting. Use visuals only when they help you reinforce important points or simplify data.
- Watch your language. The idea is to communicate your message persuasively, not to impress the audience with your extensive vocabulary or mastery of educational jargon. Use simple words and keep your sentences short. Avoid education jargon and acronyms unless they are essential to

your presentation. If you use acronyms, be sure to explain them in your speech and your handouts.

Speak clearly, but do not be afraid to use contractions. Unless your daily speech is normally contraction free, trying to avoid using any contractions will make your speech sound stilted.

We are all guilty of peppering our speech, formal or informal, with those little fillers such as "You know," "In other words," "Am I making myself clear," and the old standby, "To make a long story short," which, of course, never does. Try to make every word count and leave out the ones that do not.

- Watch your body language. Nonverbal communication such as facial expressions and body language can contradict what the presenter is saying. Avoid body language that sends negative messages such as folding your arms in front of your chest or pointing your finger at the audience, or facial expressions such as smirking and frowning when speaking or listening to the audience's questions and comments.

Practice in front of a mirror or, if possible, set up a video camera and tape yourself. Ask a colleague to sit in on one of your presentations and then give you feedback on your nonverbal communication.

Select public speakers carefully. Just because an individual likes to talk, it does not necessarily mean that he is a good presenter. I once worked with a man who was attractive, personable, and always eager to make presentations. There was one problem. When he felt intellectually threatened, he would make up words that he thought made him sound more eloquent. The result was embarrassing. Speakers dealing with controversial subjects should be able to handle a critical or demanding audience without losing their composure or confidence. Watch out for people who crave being in the spotlight. They can turn a 20-minute presentation into 40 minutes of self-admiration.

Publicize your Speakers Bureau with a list of presentation topics through your website, press releases, or letters to the program organizers of local organizations. If an issue is, or is likely to be, of public interest, prepare a brief presentation and let local organizations know that the school has someone who is available to speak about the subject.

The opportunity to speak before a group is also an opportunity to listen. Allow ample time for questions after the presentation. If the function includes a reception or meal, allow time for the speaker to socialize with attendees. If the organization used a sign-in sheet, ask for a copy to create a list of those who attended and put them in the school's database. After the presentation, the presenter should write down any ideas and comments about the presentation while they are still fresh in her mind. Writing down impressions or special details on the back of business cards can help to personalize future communication. Periodically, meet with members of the Speakers Bureau to exchange ideas, share experiences, and discuss improvements to current presentations or thoughts for new ones.

DISPELLING EDUCATION "MYTHS"

Education in this country has enough challenges without adding misinformation to the mix. Public schools, in particular, are often the target of misinformation which is often accepted as true without verification.

At a dinner party, a man who did not know that I worked for a public school district began complaining vociferously about how school districts waste the "huge" amounts of tax money they receive on administration. I asked him if he knew how school districts were funded in our state, how those funds were allocated to districts, and what percentage of district funds was spent on administration. He did not. And, he was quite surprised to learn how misinformed he was. I was able to give him the facts because I work in a school district; but, I once had the same misperceptions as he.

Myths about education based on misinformation exist and there are groups eager to use such myths to advance their own agendas. If you are a school which has experienced widespread misperceptions, be proactive in addressing them. Information is available on the Internet to help you. Use a meta-search engine such as Google! to find sites that provide list of myths with the facts to dispel them. Use them, as appropriate, in newsletters, presentations, social media, on your fax sheet, and in brochures.

Determine what myths exist within your community. If you find mistaken beliefs that are pervasive and detrimental, create a communication piece or presentation that provides the facts necessary to correct them. Ensure that your information is clear and concise. A lengthy, complicated explanation of school funding formulas, for example, is not likely to be read or understood, and, therefore, unlikely to change the public view.

Pass out information to staff members. It is possible that even school employees assume the myths to be true because they have heard them so often.

ALL POINTS OF CONTACT SHOULD BE POSITIVE

Make a list of every point of contact with the school and honestly assess if each is customer friendly. Enlist individuals from outside the school to help you in your assessment.

Are telephones answered promptly and politely? Are employees who routinely answer telephones informed about what is going on in the school or district? Is information related to frequently asked questions readily available?

Automated telephone and online systems are great for finding out your bank balance. However, automated systems do not convey personal attention and are particularly annoying when you really do want to speak to someone. Use automated systems only if your call level is so high that having "real" people answer the phone is disruptive to work flow. If you must use automation, make it user friendly and periodically test the system for its usefulness.

Check the school's system for effectiveness by calling into the school as if you were a first-time caller. I have had my call to a school answered by an automated system that asks me to enter the extension of the person I am calling. When I cannot supply the correct extension, the system instructs me to put in the first three or four letters of the person's last name. When I enter the name of the school principal, the system tells me that the name is not in the directory! If I redial to contact the school operator, the system sends me through the same dead-end routine. In this situation, a system intended to provide efficiency is counterproductive. An ineffective system suggests that customer-friendly communication is not a priority at the school.

Is the school website easy to navigate? Does the site provide information that users want? Does it provide a way for external viewers to communicate with individuals within the school?

Is the school office easy to find? Is the school office inviting? Is the staff friendly and helpful? Is printed information readily available? Are requests for information filled promptly?

The goal is to increase the flow of communication in and out. When points of communication are positive and productive, people will use them more frequently.

KEY COMMUNICATORS ARE KEY CHANNELS

Building a core of key communicators within your community is a proactive approach to effective two-way communication. Key communicators can help the school disseminate positive, accurate information, dispel rumors and exaggerated hearsay, and be the school's eyes and ears in the community.

Select representatives from many groups within your community: minority groups, retired community, businesses, and civic organizations. Include individuals who have contact with large groups of people such as hair stylists and barbers, local tavern owners, health-care providers, and shop owners, people who have influence such as civic and business leaders, people who are active in school-related issues such as PTO/PTA and teacher organizations, and people in local activist groups. Include individuals from all socioeconomic levels, age groups, and racial backgrounds.

Include people who have been critical of the school. Critics often become vocal when they feel that their views are not considered or because they feel they are not sufficiently informed about school or district activities. Inclusion of school or district critics can help mitigate future attacks and provide an insightful perspective.

Once you have selected a list of potential key communicators, contact them with a letter describing the purpose of the key communicator program, how they can participate, and why the program is important to the school and the community. Invite them to a brief meeting to explain the program, acquaint them with the school, and introduce people within the school. Follow up the letter with a phone call and, if possible, a personal meeting.

Hold the meeting at the school so they can see the facilities and the students. Keep the meeting informal, but have information packets for them to take with them. At the meeting, explain that the purpose is two-way communication. The school will keep each of them informed about the school or district and you want them to tell you what they are hearing in the community. Assure them that their participation will not require attending meetings, sending in reports, or any activities other than what they normally do on a daily basis, that is, talking and listening to people. Assign an administrator within the school to be the key communicators' contact person whom they can call or e-mail. It is important to respond to calls and e-mails promptly; otherwise, you send a message that what they have to tell or ask you is not really important.

Keep key communicators abreast of what is happening in the school through mail-outs, e-mails, and telephone calls. In a critical situation, notify them immediately with an honest assessment of the problem or circumstances. As community leaders, they can help you diffuse negative repercussions. For example, if an investigative reporter manipulates the facts about an issue at the school in order to create a sensational story, your key communicators can help the school combat the misinformation. By writing letters to the editor, contacting other local business people, talking with their customers, and speaking with local groups, key communicators help to get the school's side of the story told.

Key communicators can also serve as a channel for incoming information. Because they are interacting with people in the community on a daily basis, key communicators can inform the school about community perceptions and potential issues. Such information allows the school to be proactive in its community relations.

How many key communicators should the school have? The answer is, as many as the school can comfortably manage. Some large school districts may have more than a hundred. A school may have 10 or 12. Keep the database of key communicators current. Replace people who are no longer interested in participating or have moved away.

Once each year send a thank you letter to each key communicator. Ask for any suggestions, comments, or criticisms of the program and request names of anyone they think could be a good key communicator. Make sure they are informed about school events which they might like to attend.

A key to a successful key communicator program is trust. Ensure that information you provide to key communicators is accurate. Never use them to create hype and do not provide them with slanted information to put the school in a better light. Just one incident of a breach of trust can wreck valuable relationships and deprive the school or district of an indispensable resource.

The importance of effective communication cannot be overly stressed. However, effective communication takes effort in thought and action. It is sometimes better to say nothing than to say it badly. Spend time carefully crafting your communication whether it is verbal or nonverbal, written or spoken, interpersonal, group, or mass communication.

GOOD NEWS, BAD NEWS

Life is full of good and bad news. When the news is good, make sure everyone can enjoy the glow of good feelings. A grant for a new program, outstanding academic achievement, teacher recognition, and athletic victories should be reasons for celebration by everyone. The teacher who achieved special recognition did not do it in a vacuum. The football team does well when it feels the support of the student body. All good things should be recognized in some way. Find as many ways as you can to say, "Job, well done!" These are great opportunities for building a positive community feeling among all employees.

And then there is the bad news. These range from employee cutbacks to employee reprimands. One reason people hate to be the bearer of bad news is that they are afraid they are going to make a mess of it. It's bad enough already. Below are some suggestions to help ease the anxiety.

- If the news will affect many people such as a layoff or school closing, it should be dealt with as quickly as possible. It is difficult to keep such news secret and the rumor mill will be operating at full tilt.
- Deliver the news in person even if it requires a group meeting. Sending out some kind of form letter or e-mail is disrespectful. People should have the opportunity to ask questions and make comments within reason.
- Explain what you know; do not speculate on what you do not know.

- Keep your announcement clear and factual without the use of euphemisms and false reassurances.
- If possible, the news should be delivered by the person or persons responsible for making the decision.
- If you know, explain the what, when, how, and why of the situation.
- Have information available regarding any assistance such as severance packages, job search assistance, or training opportunities.

If you have to deliver bad news to an individual due to poor performance or unacceptable behavior the same type of rules applies. Get to the point quickly. This is not the time to chat about the recent family reunion or last night's baseball game. Be clear about what you know has happened and what needs to happen. Give the employee time to absorb the news and an opportunity to state his case. Listen carefully. Give specific examples of why you feel your actions are necessary and have any backup data or information available.

Communication is so important to your marketing effort, it is essential that sufficient time and resources be spent ensuring that your messages are effective. The key is knowing your audiences and structuring your message in a way that they find appealing, credible, and persuasive.

Success Story

John J. Herrera Elementary

Marketing Makes a Difference

John J. Herrera Elementary School, Houston, Texas, is an example of how a well-executed marketing effort can benefit a school's students, staff members, and community.

The level of excellence achieved by the students and staff of John J. Herrera Elementary contradicts the stereotypical view of its student demographics. The student population is 96 percent Hispanic (45 percent Limited English Proficiency), 95.5 percent Free/Reduced Lunch, 51 percent At-Risk, with a mobility rate of 21 percent. Yet, the school ranks as an Exemplary School, the highest rating granted by the Texas Education Agency (TEA).

In addition to teaching experience and a Masters of Education, Herrera Principal Hector Rodríguez has an M.B.A. and several years in private business. His experience in the private sector gives Mr. Rodríguez an appreciation of the power of a well-organized and focused marketing effort.

To Mr. Rodríguez, marketing is not an option. "We have a different environment from past years regarding how we are accountable for what we are doing in our schools. We are also performing in a more competitive and sophisticated environment. To succeed in the type of environment, schools need to have a complete understanding of what they are doing and how they are doing it. Then they need to communicate, and, in some cases, educate their communities about what they are doing. Finally, every school needs to understand how similar and different their services are from those of other schools and learn how to highlight their uniqueness."

"Marketing is not something we do occasionally," stated Mr. Rodríguez, "because marketing is about product improvement, customer satisfaction, and effective communication, and these are things we are always striving toward.

An effective marketing program should come naturally in everything you do within school activities. It is an understanding that the final product is student growth directly and staff and community growth indirectly. A positive culture sells itself!"

Principal Rodríguez knows that no amount of marketing can substitute for an inferior product. The highest marketing and academic priority for administration and staff is creating the best academic products possible. A good product is one that meets the needs and wants of the customer: an outstanding product is one that *exceeds* the customers' needs and wants. The administration and staff dedicate considerable thought to academic programs that not only shape the students' present and future success, but also benefit the community at large.

The marketing approach creates an atmosphere in which individuals are always thinking, "How can we create a better product?" At Herrera, the administration and staff continually strive to create a product that is excellent in quality and innovative in its approach to learning. Part of the marketing strategy is to combine the latest technology with inventive programs that continually improve the learning environment. The school is dedicated to finding creative ways for students and teachers to venture beyond the boundaries of textbooks and to search the world electronically for new ideas. This approach has made Herrera a preferred school for students and parents.

One of Herrera's outstanding products is its two-way language immersion program in grades kindergarten through second. Limited English Proficient students and monolingual English students are together in classes where they develop fluency in both languages as well as a strong foundation in academic areas. The ultimate goal is to produce bilingual and bi-literate students throughout the school. This type of program is attractive not only to parents, most of whom are Spanish speaking, but also to businesses in a state where being bilingual is a valuable asset.

The school's technology-driven curriculum transcends the standard computer-based learning. One example is the daily morning show transmitted from the school's broadcast center. The show is a means to communicate important information, recognize achievements, encourage confidence, and build self-esteem. A typical morning includes comments from the principal, a weather report and the lunch menu delivered by the students, and recognition of student accomplishments and birthdays. The program always closes with the school pledge, "Today, I will respect my teacher, my peers, and my school. I will do more than is expected of me."

The daily broadcast provides more than a means to communicate information within the school. The program helps students to develop technical expertise early in their academic careers while teaching valuable lessons in organization, project management, research, design, and communication.

Students have used the school's technology to address issues important to them and the community. Many of the students have relatives in the military, some serving in Iraq. The school wanted a way to lessen the fears and concerns of the students. Students and faculty created a video that incorporated excerpts from student essays on "Why I Like America" and pictures of relatives in the military with patriotic symbols and music. The video had a significant effect on the students' ability to cope with the uncertainty and apprehension they felt about what they see and hear in the media.

The high-quality programs at Herrera Elementary allow the school to position itself as an organization that takes the community's needs and wants seriously and is meeting them successfully. The ultimate product of Herrera, however, is the student who is enhanced significantly by the quality programs the school provides. From the earliest grade levels, students are acquiring language and technical proficiency that will benefit their lives and the economics of the community.

Explaining his philosophy, Principal Rodríguez said, "Marketing is developing a product or service and its concept. In essence, you understand your product and create a concept around it. For example, at Herrera Elementary, we want to communicate quality education which is based on caring for children, relationships with our community, use of technology, and language development and maintenance, both Spanish and English."

Mr. Rodríguez knows that the environment where the product is delivered is important in marketing. The school's emphasis on using technology to maximize the learning experience is evident. To utilize fully the benefits of the broadcast studio, every classroom has a VideoLAN server, a DVD player, and a television monitor. There is one computer for every two students.

Mr. Rodríguez also believes that schools can and must strike a balance between a safe environment and a welcoming one. Schools need to protect their children. At the same time parents, volunteers, or community partners must feel welcome or they will not participate. At Herrera, the welcome is apparent before the visitor enters the front door. The school grounds are clean and tidy and visitor parking is available at the school entrance. The school interior is immaculate. The staff implements security measures in ways that do not make visitors feel like intruders. The atmosphere is one of high energy and activity with a purpose.

An environment that represents excellence attracts top-notch people. In return, these people are motivated to sustain and cultivate the level of excellence that makes the environment so attractive. The marketing effort at Herrera is successful in attracting talented people and in utilizing their participation to promote the level of excellence.

All professional staff members are qualified for gifted and talented education. Last year, the school lost none of its quality teachers. Principal

Rodríguez attributes the school's ability to recruit and retain quality staff to an internal atmosphere of respect, high standards, and professionalism. The high level of professionalism mixed with a heavy measure of enthusiasm and pride creates an environment that attracts quality people.

The level of achievement and pride exhibited by the school's staff and students also attracts parents. Parents and the community, in general, are eager to be a part of the school's positive atmosphere. The school encourages participation in various ways. Herrera uses traditional methods, which include VIPS (Volunteers in Public Schools), PTA, and an "Open Door" policy for parents; however, it also uses more unconventional methods.

Each year, Herrera hosts its annual Fathers' Night, where between 100 and 150 fathers (and some mothers) attend presentations on school and community issues during a catered dinner. This is an effort to target an important segment of the population that traditionally does not participate in such events. The school makes the evening fun for the fathers, each of whom receives a book to "autograph" and present to his child as a gift. To add special interest, fathers can win door prizes, such as tools and sports equipment.

Another such event is the "Día del Nino" celebration, during which the PTA and community members and business partners come together to celebrate childhood. This event relates to the Mexican tradition of the Día del Nino, celebrated every year on April 30.

The school holds celebrations, often featuring traditional Mexican Mariachi music, throughout the year to recognize achievements. After the state-mandated test, the school celebrates with a carnival for the children. A Mothers' Day celebration recognizes mothers and provides certificates of appreciation to the school's VIPS.

The school conducts weekly parenting sessions that address community and family issues, as well as developmental considerations for fifth graders moving on to middle school. When needed, teachers bring parents into classrooms to sit with their children to help them establish long-term goals and evaluate their children's academic and behavioral performance.

Another annual event, which takes place after the beginning of the school year, is a field trip for parents and their children to the Museum of Health. This event involves parents in their children's learning, introduces parents and students to the museum, and increases parents' awareness of health issues concerning their children and themselves.

The after-school program at Herrera is designed to assist the working parent. Students remain in school under supervision until 5:30 p.m. when parents can collect their children. The children experience enrichment activities, both academic and cultural. This has become a critical program in the development of strong relationships with those working parents.

The school creates an awareness of its presence in the community by participating in community parades and other civic events. School tours are scheduled on Friday mornings from January to May, a time when parents are most likely to be selecting a school for the next year.

Herrera has developed strong relationships with many community partners, including the City of Houston, Museum of Fine Arts, YMCA, police and fire departments, and the neighborhood Fiesta food market, who help with children's festivals and other events. Partners donate items as door prizes for the Fathers' Night, or become involved as guest speakers for career days and/or Fathers' Night.

In other situations, organizations have helped by awarding grants for special projects, such as the YES Grant ($2,000 for use in purchasing safety equipment) and the Houston Rocket's $1,000 grant for field trips for kindergarten students. Herrera has enjoyed the Harris County grant, which has provided more than $200,000 for after-school program over the past several years, and the Capital Investment grant, which provides over $40,000 to spend with parents and teachers.

Many parents who have skills in the crafts have donated their time and resources to the school. Some of these relationships have resulted in donations for faculty luncheons or holiday celebrations. The participation of individuals, businesses, and organizations from the community creates an encouraging climate within the school.

Mr. Rodríguez expresses the importance of involving everyone in the marketing effort when he says, "Our teachers and our parents are our best salespeople." Their commitment and participation are powerful testimonials.

Mr. Rodríguez is aware that everything, even the smallest thing, about the school creates an impression and communicates a message. "Simply, we want everyone to know what sets Herrera Elementary apart from the crowd: what make us different and unique." The school uses a number of mediums to create an awareness of the school and its accomplishments.

The school uniform is a polo-type shirt or t-shirt with the Herrera Elementary School logo and "We ♥ Our Children" on the front. On one sleeve is printed "Exemplary School 2002–2003." The uniform is a tangible, public announcement of the school's pride in its accomplishments. In addition to being an "advertisement" for the high quality of the school, the uniform creates a sense of belonging and special membership among the students. In turn, students are more likely to give extra effort toward maintaining the excellence of the school and their place in it.

The school brochure is a simple, concise, and straightforward expression of the school's achievements, programs, and mission. In addition to a photograph of the school, the cover lists the school's academic standing since 1995. The first thing the reader sees is a clear, objective affirmation of the school's commitment to excellence. The brochure text communicates the school's emphasis on excellence, technology, and foreign language development and provides information such as educational strategies and programs and a profile of teacher demographics.

The website reaches out to the community by going beyond supplying school information that students and parents want to know. It draws parents to the site by providing links to valuable information that can help families in their daily lives. Herrera has recently developed a school DVD that highlights much of the spirit and programs at Herrera Elementary. This DVD is used for special guests and visitors, or specific groups with interest in the school. The school will use this technique to target potential business partners (in marketing terms, "selected segments" of interest to our school).

The community around Herrera Elementary is not wealthy, but Rodriguez believes that the community deserves a level of education and resulting student achievement equal to schools in more affluent neighborhoods. Principal Rodríguez and the staff members at Herrera Elementary are delivering a product that is of the highest quality. In return, the community gives value back to the school. The community pays taxes, but value does not always involve money. A high level of parental involvement and community support adds value that helps the school maintain a high level of quality. The community, in turn, believes it is receiving value for the price it pays in taxes, contributions of time and money, and support of the school's goals. A price the community pays willingly.

Appendix B

Success Story

Colorado Springs School District 11

Electronic Dialogue: A Means to Greater Community Loyalty

With over 30,000 students, School District 11 is the seventh largest school district in Colorado and the largest school district in the Pikes Peak region. The district includes 38 elementary schools (grades K–5); one K-8 school; nine middle schools (grades 6–8); five high schools (grades 9–12); five alternative schools and/or programs; one digital high school; six charter schools; and adult and family education programs. Nestled at the foot of Pikes Peak and the front range of the Colorado Rockies, Colorado Springs, with a population of about 400,000, would appear to be an idyllic location in which to raise and educate children; and it is.

However, District 11 faced challenges related to the inner city characteristics of the area that it serves, which is the older, more established part of the city. Many of the people in District 11's community are retired or no longer have school-age children, giving them less motivation to vote for additional taxes or mill levies in support of District 11.

Suburban expansion had hit Colorado Springs, like most cities, resulting in many of the more affluent families moving away from the center of the city into school districts which now surround District 11. This had limited the district's ability to expand its service area and reintegrate some of these newer neighborhoods. This kept the district from being able to expand its taxable base, while the property values have tended to trail the rate of growth of suburban school districts. In addition, as the oldest school district in the Colorado Springs area, District 11 had some of the oldest schools and facilities, which require a lot of maintenance and upkeep and in many instances replacement.

Even with these fiscal constraints, District 11 provided a high quality of educational services to its community and had been recognized for its efforts and results in implementing quality and continuous improvement systems. The challenges faced by the district, however, related in many ways to how the district and its educational services and staff members were perceived by the parents and taxpayers of the community.

By the Spring of 2002, District 11 had already deployed numerous online programs to help the district administration and individual campuses interact with the community more effectively. These include a library search system (SIRSI) for finding and reserving library resources throughout the district; a school lunch system to allow students and parents to purchase school lunches online; a community education enrollment system; Teacher Connect, Parent Connect, and Student Connect, which allowed these stakeholders to monitor, collaborate, and seek answers regarding individual class curriculum and assignments as well as information about individual students.

While many of these applications were part of an overall community relations effort using the Internet, the district was only beginning to look at online tools for marketing and customer service functions at the district level. In early 2002, the communications function was receiving proportionally greater emphasis because of the failure earlier in the decade to pass a bond issue which would have helped the district upgrade many of its older facilities.

District 11 had an active communications and community relations office headed by Ms. Elaine Naleski, and the district website contained a broad range of policy and procedural content and went several levels deep with 'sub-webs' for different departments within the district. In addition, the site provided links to many of the operational systems mentioned above.

However, the District 11 Communications and Community Relations Office was only beginning to look at ways to streamline their own communication processes and use the Web more interactively to improve responsiveness to the community. As part of her effort to convince the Board of Education to take action regarding an online community relations system, Ms. Naleski identified several benefits, including faster, more efficient, and more convenient delivery of information; customer friendliness (24 hours-a-day availability); quality (e.g., accuracy) of information; the ability to "push out" important information; the ability to track data within the system; and the need to track opinions of the community through online surveying.

Ms. Naleski made a persuasive argument, but there were still concerns about utilizing the Internet for community relations programs, primarily based on a Board of Education perception that it might be seen as less personal than other channels. In the end, Ms. Naleski was able to overcome these concerns because everyone acknowledged the need to take some action to improve the community relations program. From a financial perspective, hiring more staff members to handle these programs was not cost-effective; therefore, after almost a year of internal discussion and review, the board gave the D-11 Communications Office the go-ahead to find an Internet-based community relations tool.

One of the first processes identified for improvement was the e-mail system that came through the district's website. There were several links on the site where users could click and send an e-mail to the district. The vast majority of these e-mails landed in the inbox of one person in the District 11 Communications Office who then had to track down the answers from a knowledgeable person or department and respond to the users. This process resulted in a relatively long response time, redundant responses to the same questions, and a procedural bottleneck because questions could be processed only as fast as one person could track down the answers.

To address this bottleneck, the District 11 Communications Office decided to develop an online, automated program called "D-11 Answers" that would provide a knowledgebase of frequently asked questions (FAQs) on their website. The system would also direct questions to the correct person or department within the district most likely to know the answers, automatically updating the knowledgebase with the answers once staff responded. In addition, the D-11 Communications Office needed a way to track response time and unanswered questions.

When considering options for the system, Ms. Naleski's team had to decide whether to wait on the Information Technology (IT) Department to develop such a program or go outside for assistance. After much internal discussion, it was decided to go with an outside system. Since the D-11 Communications Office did not want the project to depend on availability of IT resources to install a commercial system on the district's own servers, they chose a hosted solution. The hosted system, called "ezCommunicator," had the knowledgebase function and also included several other interactive components. The D-11 Communications Office could have chosen a system which had only knowledgebase functions, but they recognized that they would probably want to expand to use of other online interactive components. Having those components available in a single integrated system made it easier to deploy these other functions on an as-needed basis.

"One of the first and largest challenges we faced was getting buy-in from the rest of the departments within the district office once we had board approval to proceed with the project," explained Elaine Naleski. Aside from getting IT commitment to the technical side of the D-11 Answers system, the D-11 Communications Office had to persuade, and in some cases cajole, different departments to take on responsibility for responding to questions in their areas of expertise.

With D-11 Answers deployed, the D-11 Communications Office has been able to track the trend in usage of the system, for both viewing questions and posting questions. They have also, from a quality improvement aspect, been able to track the response time to questions coming through the system and have seen a steady improvement to a level of approximately one business day, which was an original target for quality.

Since November 2003, when the above information was compiled and presented at an international education conference, District 11 has continued to expand their use of the Internet as part of their communications and community relations programs.

In early 2004, the District 11 administration was beginning to search for ways to market particular high schools within the district that were losing students and suffering from poor community perception. As part of the community outreach and marketing efforts at these high schools, the D-11 Communications Office decided to deploy the same system used at the district level on the school websites so that these schools can begin to utilize more interactive, Internet-based tools to strengthen community loyalty.

The D-11 Communications Office has gradually broadened use of the interactive tools within the ezCommunicator system and now distributes electronic newsletters to various subscribers of the system. They use the survey and online poll capabilities to gain quick insights into community interest and positions on certain issues, and they provide users with the opportunity to subscribe to various announcement groups and categories of interest.

In November 2004, District 11 ran another bond election and was successful in getting voter approval for $132 million for capital improvements across the district. While many people were involved and many other methods were used to get out the message about the value of the bond to the community, District 11 was able to make effective use of their D-11 Answers system to respond to questions submitted by the voters in the community and to take periodic surveys and polls to gauge support.

"We've learned that we could have gained more benefit earlier in using the system if we had planned out how we would apply each of the features to its fullest effect. We also learned that we should have involved more people, including end users, in the process of defining our requirements in order to get their buy-in up-front," said Ms. Naleski. "Using the Internet as part of our communications strategy is a process of continuous advancement. We're always looking for ways to use the Web site and e-mail to refine our message to the community and improve the community's perception of us as a responsive school district committed to the highest level of quality education. Implementing an Internet community relations system has been, and continues to be, a journey for us—not a single event."

Appendix C

Success Story

Community Connections for All Students/Arts Education Matters

As part of their effort to benefit their city, a major Houston philanthropic organization, The Robert and Janice McNair Foundation, approached the Houston Heights Association and Houston Independent School District's then North Central District with an offer to establish a partnership designed to improve the quality of life in the historic Heights neighborhood, located five miles northwest of downtown Houston. The resulting agreement, "Community Connections for all Students," began a three-year partnership in which the McNair Foundation pledged $1.5 million to improve school fine arts programs, invest in adult and parent education programs, technology, health education, and to generally improve the quality of life in the community. Through a close collaboration between Joanie Haley, McNair Foundation Executive Director, and Heights resident Jerri Workman of the Greater Heights Education Partnership, "Community Connections" became a model in collaborative initiatives so successful that the McNair Foundation chose to continue its support beyond the original three-year commitment.

A major goal for the school fine arts program component was to create an initiative funded by the McNair Foundation that would have the greatest impact possible on arts education by facilitating partnerships between Houston-area arts organizations and inner city public schools. At the time, the need was great. A variety of factors, mainly financial, had resulted in the elimination of some fine arts teaching positions and reductions in many fine arts program budgets. Six elementary schools, that served approximately 1,500 students, had no fine arts programs at all. Of those elementary schools that did offer fine arts classes, instruction was available only 40–50 minutes once a week. As a result, arts programs on the secondary level were few or nonexistent. There was little opportunity for students to experience the fine arts on a meaningful level.

In addition to providing program support, the McNair Foundation also provided matching funds to establish a Coordinator of Fine Arts position to oversee all aspects of the initiative. After an extensive candidate search, R. Neal Wiley was hired as coordinator. Mr. Wiley had 25 years of experience as a fine arts educator in public schools, both as an instructor and as an administrator. He served on the Board of Directors of Chrysalis Dance Company, InterActive Theater, Mercury Baroque Ensemble, was on the Education Committee of Young Audiences of Houston, and served as a member of Houston Community College-Central's Visual and Performing Arts Committee. Mr. Wiley was also a consultant to several local and state fine arts organizations. These credentials provided the expertise and contacts to establish a successful program within the original allotted time frame of three years. The program began with five Houston-area arts partner organizations providing programs to schools, and grew to include 15 arts and education organizations in all fine arts disciplines.

Mr. Wiley knew that with a limited amount of time and money, he had to get the most bang for the bucks he had. It was important early on to convey to teachers, administrators, and parents the many benefits of arts programs. Of utmost importance were recent studies indicating that when students have access to fine arts programs, learning is enhanced and achievement is increased. For students who become active in the arts, the development of patience, persistence, discipline, and a sense of accomplishment are benefits that will serve them throughout their lives.

Mr. Wiley had first-hand knowledge of how exposure to things new and wonderful can affect a child's world. "When we go to Jones Hall (Houston's symphony hall), I always try to run ahead of the children, so I can see the expressions on their faces when they come into the hall's spacious entry," explained Mr. Wiley. "Their looks of wonder and surprise tell you that something exceptional is happening. And our teachers report that learning that one must be very quiet in the symphony hall or during a theatrical performance has resulted in positive behavior modification in the classroom."

Activities in the first phase were also devoted to getting schools and parents more actively involved. To get schools involved, program logistics had to be easy. Mr. Wiley knew that a program involving a complicated process or continual effort would not be well received. At the beginning of each school year, a presentation was made to all principals and each one received a fine arts packet describing the activities participating arts organizations were willing to provide. One request form listed *all* activities. Principals simply checked off the activities they wanted for the year. All bookings and communication went through Mr. Wiley's office. In some cases, the schools provided the transportation and the organizations provided the program. In other instances, organizations brought their programs to the school. "I have yet to encounter a principal who did not value fine arts and want the arts in their school," said Mr. Wiley. "Their frustration, and mine, was how to pay for arts programs in the face of declining budgets and in the current atmosphere of high-stakes testing. The approach we have taken, one of collaboration and thinking outside the proverbial box, has taken some time to implement, but the results are undeniable."

Getting the parents' support for the project required overcoming cultural, financial, and logistical challenges to fine arts participation. Mr. Wiley felt the best way to communicate with parents was direct involvement through an arts event. "School events, such as PTA/O programs involving students, are a good way to attract parents to the school," says Mr. Wiley. Parents were also invited to be chaperones on fine arts field trips. In addition to these initiatives, it was decided that an annual community-based signature arts event be held to bring schools and community members together for a special day of fine arts activities.

As a result, an annual Festival of the Arts was established and held each spring on the John H. Reagan High School campus. Funded by the McNair Foundation, the Houston Heights Association, and several other local businesses and civic groups, the first Festival attracted over 1,000 people. Parents who had never come to the school before were there. The Festival, which showcased hundreds of student visual and performing arts experiences, also included representatives of the local fine arts community, giving the event an added level of significance. Attendance and participation increased steadily every year thereafter, and plans were made to hold additional Festivals at the other high schools within Houston ISD's Northwest District.

Since the project began, over 350 campus-based student education and outreach programs have been presented. Over 6,000 students have attended performances at the Alley Theatre and in Jones Hall in downtown Houston. Approximately 30 campus-based artist-in-residence programs have been created for area schools, both during the regular instructional day and in after-school programs. The residencies allow artists from the arts partner organizations to work with students on specific projects over a greater period of time, typically several weeks to an entire school year, thereby providing opportunities for students to experience the arts at a depth and complexity previously unavailable to them.

"We're moving away from the 'one-shot' arts experience," explained Mr. Wiley. "We, of course, value individual performances, and we are constantly developing and improving collaboratively-designed integrated lesson plans, pre- and post- performance activities for students, etc., that both enhance the arts experiences as well as tie the experiences to other subject areas. We find that teachers and principals appreciate this a great deal."

Over 150 teachers have been trained in art integration techniques. Foundation donations have been leveraged to bring in approximately $40,000 in additional funds from state and county organizations. By the end of the third year, "Community Connections" was a resounding success, and discussions were initiated to explore ways to expand and replicate the model in other Houston ISD schools.

At a time when diminishing resources were forcing schools to cut back or eliminate their fine arts programs, Joe Nuber, Superintendent of the Northwest Administrative District (NWD) in Houston, was determined to maintain an arts presence in the 26 Title I schools in his district, which served some 19,000 economically disadvantaged inner city children. With plans to expand the original 16 school fine arts initiative to the entire NWD, Mr. Nuber made the bold step of establishing a Director of Fine Arts position for the Northwest District, and chose Mr. Wiley to continue to implement and expand to scale the established programs. A key factor in expansion was to secure the continued support of the McNair Foundation.

A bilingual parent survey and a campus principal needs assessment were prepared by the NWD Fine Arts Department and administered to determine levels of need and interest. The bilingual parent survey was administered by participating elementary schools and measured the interest in each fine arts discipline—art, dance, music, and theater. The needs assessment done by NWD principals asked them to project their anticipated fine arts course offerings for the coming academic years, as well as to identify areas of weakness or need in fine arts course offerings. Cumulative results of both the parent interest survey and the principal needs assessment indicated overwhelming support and a clear need for arts education programs in NWD schools beyond what the schools alone could provide.

In response to these survey and needs assessment results, not only did the McNair Foundation continue to support the collaborative fine arts model program, it *increased* the level of support for the second phase of the program. This second phase was called "Arts Education Matters," a groundbreaking and comprehensive program to incrementally integrate arts education into other core subject areas and daily activities in all of the 26 schools in the NWD over the next five years. Schools were expected to fund a gradually increasing percentage of the overall cost of programs on their campus. Local businesses were sought as collaborative partners with NWD schools to financially support fine arts programs at the schools in their neighborhood. Arts Education Matters (AEM) had four major components:

1. Campus-based **performances** for students, faculty and staff
2. Campus-based **artist-in-residence** and/or **workshop** experiences
3. **Field trips** to Arts Partners' venues
4. Comprehensive **curriculum integration staff development** experiences for non-fine arts classroom teachers

All four components were a continuation of the original "Community Connections" initiative. AEM's goal was to expand the components to scale in all 26 NWD schools. Additionally, a significant increase in the scope of teacher training through arts curriculum integration staff development opportunities for non-fine arts classroom teachers was a major program component. Without the funds to hire additional fine arts instructors, the goal was to infuse the arts into the schools through non-fine arts teachers.

The first step was AEM's "renewal" process in which teachers were renewed by discovering the wealth of ways in which the arts can have a positive impact upon students' lives and learning. Renewal is an intrinsically motivated approach to self-improvement. Through AEM, educators had the opportunity to learn creative strategies for reaching more students in deep and meaningful ways. Teachers were able to enroll in arts curriculum integration workshops for professional development and gifted and talented credits.

One arts partner in particular, the Museum of Fine Arts, Houston (MFAH), provided the majority of the arts curriculum integration training, and also provided follow-up support in the classroom through an arts curriculum integration program, *Learning Through Art*. The program was designed by teachers for teachers to show them how to incorporate art instruction into other subjects. Those who completed the training received curriculum kits with integrated lesson plans.

To date, more than 150 teachers have gone through the training and renewal process. The response was so great that participation had to be limited. "The MFAH teacher training program, along with their vast Kinder Teacher Resource Center, has been the single strongest component of our overall fine arts initiative," according to Mr. Wiley. "We view *Learning Through Art* as *the* model for arts integration in public schools."

Mr. Wiley was particularly proud of one approach to showcasing students' artwork, the *Art Space* in the Northwest District's administration building, a permanent gallery installation created with help from the Museum of Fine Arts, Houston. Through the use of special framing, lighting, and small plaques with artwork titles and student artist's name, *Art Space* displayed selected pieces of children's art as though it were in a museum setting.

Mr. Wiley understood that organizations that donate time and money want to see results. To provide independent assessment, Dr. Cynthia Herbert, based in Austin, Texas, served as program evaluator. Formerly Executive Director of the Texas Alliance for Education and the Arts, which was the Texas member of the Kennedy Center Alliance for Arts Education Network, Dr. Herbert had over 30 years of experience in arts education and was considered an expert in her field. The project was evaluated quantitatively by the number of and type of programs and services delivered to schools, number of children served, number of teachers trained in arts integration techniques, number of schools hosting pilot programs, and the number of hours of programs and services. A random sampling of teachers and students participating in the program was used to ascertain positive changes in school attendance and test scores, as well as decreased numbers of disciplinary actions and referrals. Qualitative evaluation involved responses to age-and language-appropriate questionnaires for students; teacher, school administrator, and parent surveys; and observations of program activities by key project personnel.

"I cannot say enough about the generosity and vision of The Robert and Janice McNair Foundation and its Executive Director Joanie Haley," said Mr. Wiley. "Over the years, many well-meaning education initiatives have failed because they were abandoned after a few years for a variety of reasons, lack of sustaining funding being chief among them. The McNair Foundation, Houston ISD's Northwest District administration, and our arts partners know that one must stay the course in order to see measurable results. This is especially true in the arts. Exposure to the arts affects people in evolutionary stages, something that cannot easily be measured as yearly progress on a standardized test. The indirect effect is there. You just have to know how to look for it."

Arts Education Matters is a success story about building partnerships, bringing key stakeholders together, and facilitating discussions to build consensus over time—all with the needs of inner city children in mind. The power of AEM is in the belief that the arts are *essential* to the quality of life, both in and out of school, not a "frill" or an "extra." "At the end of the day," stated Mr. Wiley, "we (AEM) must be the advocates for our children and their families for arts education. If we don't speak out for them, who will?"

Conclusion

The environment in which schools function will continue to change. Demands for higher standards, greater competition from alternative forms of education, increased need for community support, and challenges in recruiting high-quality personnel require that schools and districts have the methods, materials, and mindset to be aware of and to meet the needs, wants, and expectations of their internal and external stakeholders. An organized marketing effort will help schools accomplish that.

As stated in the beginning of this book, many schools are already marketing, whether they call it that or not. Often what they lack is a strategy to maximize their efforts. I hope this book will assist schools in initiating, implementing, and maintaining an effective marketing plan to mutually benefit themselves and their communities and thereby enhance the learning experience for all students.

About the Author

Johanna M. Lockhart has extensive experience in marketing and public relations in the private sector. For more than 10 years, she used that experience in her position as Manager of the Department of Marketing and Business Development at the Houston Independent School District. Ms. Lockhart has created and presented marketing workshops to hundreds of school and district administrators and has made presentations at state and national conferences.

In 2014, Ms. Lockhart retired from the school district and is now launching a new endeavor. Her website, *marketyourschool.net*, is a result of feedback from readers of the first edition of the book. The goal is to provide marketing assistance, through consulting and workshops, to public, private, charter, or parochial schools anywhere in the country or abroad.

Ms. Lockhart holds a Bachelor of Arts, magna cum laude, in languages and has studied in England, Germany, Spain, and Mexico. She also holds a Master of Arts in communication/public relations.

Ms. Lockhart now resides in Austin, Texas. She may be reached through her website, *marketyourschool.net*